Postmodernism
for Beginners

by James N. Powell

Writers and Readers Publishing, Inc.
P.O. Box 461, Village Station
New York, NY 10014

Writers and Readers Limited
35 Britannia Row
London N1 8QH
Tel: 0171 226 3377
Fax:: 0171 359 1454
e-mail: begin@writersandreaders.com

A Writers and Readers Documentary Comic Book

Copyright © 1998
ISBN 0-86316-188-X Trade
1 2 3 4 5 6 7 8 9 0

Printed in Finland by WSOY

Beginners Documentary Comic Books are published by Writers and Readers Publishing, Inc. Its trademark, consisting of the words "For Beginners, Writers and Readers Documentary Comic Books" and the Writers and Readers logo, is registered in the U. S. Patent and Trademark Office and in other countries.

Writers and Readers

publishing FOR BEGINNERS™ books continuously since 1975

1975:Cuba •1976: Marx •1977: Lenin •1978: Nuclear Power •1979: Einstein •Freud•1980: Mao • Trotsky •1981: Capitalism •1982: Darwin• Economics • French Revolution• Marx's Kapital •Food •Ecology •1983: DNA•Ireland •1984: London • Peace •Medicine •Orwell•Reagan • Nicaragua • Black History • 1985: Mark Diary • 1986: Zen • Psychiatry • Reich • Socialism •Computers •Brecht • Elvis •1988: Architecture • Sex •JFK • Virginia Woolf•1990: Nietzsche • Plato • Malcolm X • Judaism •1991: WWII • Erotica• African History •1992: Philosophy • •Rainforests•Miles Davis •Islam• Pan Africanism •1993: Black Women • Arabs and Israel • 1994: Babies •Foucault • Heidegger •Hemingway • Classical Music •1995: Jazz •Jewish Holocaust • Health Care • Domestic Violence • Sartre •United Nations •Black Holocaust •Black Panthers • Martial Arts •History of Clowns •1996: Opera •Biology •Saussure •UNICEF •Kierkegaard •Addiction & Recovery •I Ching • Buddha •Derrida •Chomsky • McLuhan •Jung •1997: Lacan •Shakespeare • Structuralism •Che • 1998:Fanon •Adler •Ghandi • Toni Morrison

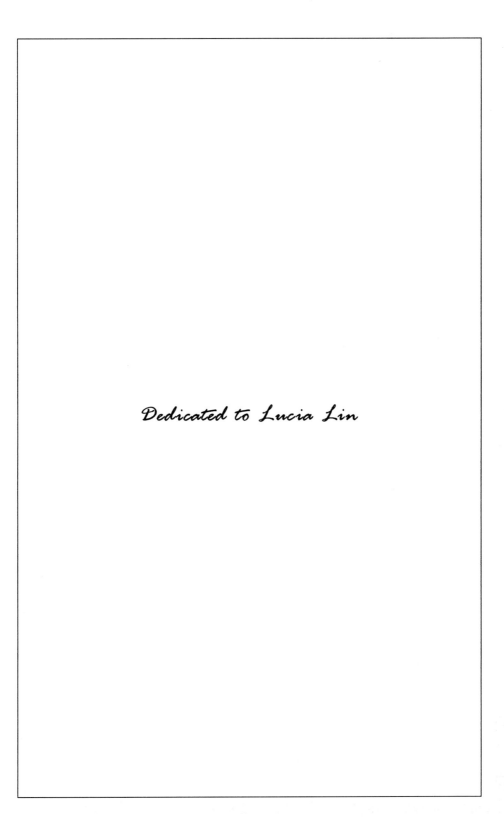

Dedicated to Lucia Lin

TABLE of CONTENTS

Introduction

An arts brochure for almost any major university might appropriately feature a photomontage representing its season of cultural offerings from around the world. The montage might feature a female dancer with an East Indian head, a male Navaho left leg, the right leg of an Afro-American modern dancer, a torso half-covered by a suit and tie, and the other half festooned with eagle feathers, with one arm displaying a sacred Tibetan hand gesture, another muscled arm pounding out a rhythm on a Japanese drum, and two more female arms in a lyrical dance pose from India.

Contrast this cultural mixing with the lives of most of the people who have lived on the planet for most of its history. Citizens of the Middle Ages and members of pre-modern tribal societies could live out their years without encountering anyone with another god, a contrary worldview, different folktales, dances or myths. If they should encounter an individual or a society that was different, then the strategy was to conquer it militarily, economically and sexually; to convert it to one's own religion; or to kill it. The very existence of the Other, the very presence of the Other, posed a threat to the supposed universality of one's own beliefs.

In the Postmodern age, however, it is difficult to get through a day without confronting many different realities. Simply turn on the TV and you might hear a World Music group singing a blend of Irish love song, Indian raga, heavy-metal anthem, Mongolian Buddhist chant—and all to the tune of peyote drums, gamelans, didgeridoos, panpipes, nose flutes, alpenhorns, sitars and tambourines. And all these sounds may be produced not by the original instrument but electronically, to a danceable reggae or hip-hop beat, and broadcast worldwide via satellite to millions of viewers—the profits going to save the Brazilian rainforest. In fact, go to a fundamentalist Islamic wedding in an Egyptian village, and the bride, surrounded by stern elders, hooded and veiled so that no intruding male gaze will pollute her—may secretly be listening to the concert,

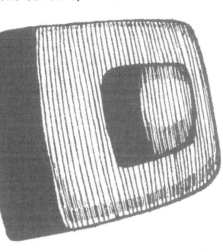

OM.
IT'S THE REAL THING.

beneath the hood, through the earphones of her miniaturized radio. She may be wearing jeans under her traditional skirt, and have a belly full of Coca-Cola.

Pick up any New Age magazine, and you will find the Mysterious and Unknown sold in a thousand forms—psychic channelings of disembodied spirits, Buddhist, Taoist and Hindu meditation techniques, Native American sweat baths, crystals and herbs, electronic meditation machines and exotic potions. Your typical New Ager sees no contradiction in attending a Quaker meeting in the morning, eating a Zen macrobiotic breakfast, sitting for Chinese Taoist meditation, eating an Indian Ayurvedic lunch, doing a Cherokee sweat before Tai Chi, munching down a soyburger for dinner, dancing in a full-moon witching ceremony with her neo-Pagan Goddess group, and then coming home and making love with her New Age boyfriend according to Hindu Tantric principles.

All the world's cultures, rituals, races, databanks,  myths and musical motifs are intermixing like a smorgasbord in an earthquake. And this hodge-podge of hybrid images is glob-al, flooding the traditional mass media, and also Cyberspace—a space ever-blossoming with new universes and realities, and which is being probed by an ever expanding population of cyberpunks and cyber-shamans who—like electronic rats burrowing sideways through a vast interconnected series of electronic sewers, cellars, passageways, caverns, gutters, and tunnels—are capable of navigating from cybersite to cybersite via an almost infinitely inter-linked catalogue of codes. In other words, we live increasingly in a world of interconnected differences—

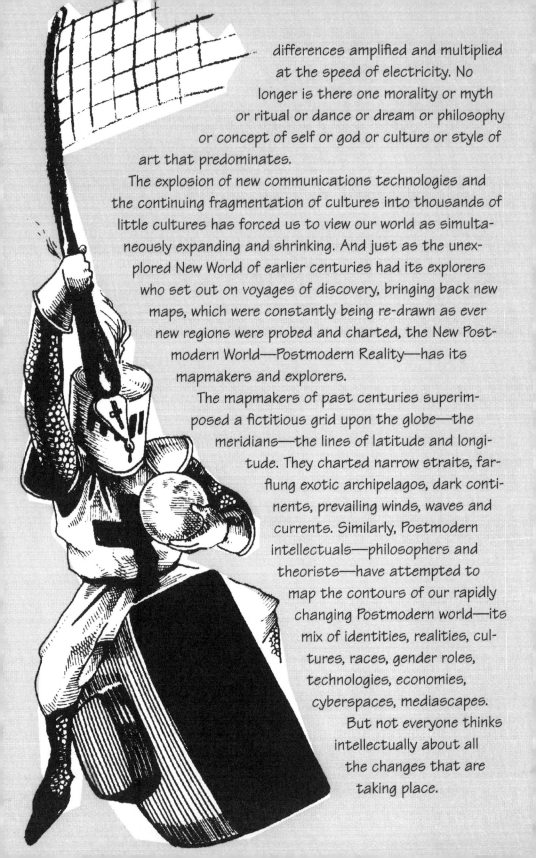

differences amplified and multiplied at the speed of electricity. No longer is there one morality or myth or ritual or dance or dream or philosophy or concept of self or god or culture or style of art that predominates.

The explosion of new communications technologies and the continuing fragmentation of cultures into thousands of little cultures has forced us to view our world as simultaneously expanding and shrinking. And just as the unexplored New World of earlier centuries had its explorers who set out on voyages of discovery, bringing back new maps, which were constantly being re-drawn as ever new regions were probed and charted, the New Postmodern World—Postmodern Reality—has its mapmakers and explorers.

The mapmakers of past centuries superimposed a fictitious grid upon the globe—the meridians—the lines of latitude and longitude. They charted narrow straits, far-flung exotic archipelagos, dark continents, prevailing winds, waves and currents. Similarly, Postmodern intellectuals—philosophers and theorists—have attempted to map the contours of our rapidly changing Postmodern world—its mix of identities, realities, cultures, races, gender roles, technologies, economies, cyberspaces, mediascapes. But not everyone thinks intellectually about all the changes that are taking place.

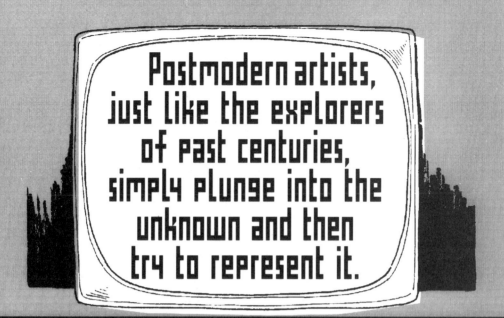

Postmodern artists, just like the explorers of past centuries, simply plunge into the unknown and then try to represent it.

These Postmodern artists or architects simply take note of the new mix of messages, symbols, cultures and media, and then create a video, song, painting or building that reflects the Postmodern condition. We will be exploring the thoughts of some of these "mapmakers" and "explorers," these Postmodern intellectuals and artists, in the pages that follow.

Post-modernese

Q **But wait a minute! If Postmodern thinkers have some really new ideas mapping the contours of our times, why haven't I heard of these ideas before?**

A A major reason is that Postmodernese is such a difficult language to understand—and most books on Postmodernism are written in this particularly obscure tongue.

For instance—let's suppose you live in the 1970s, and you want to say "The way white guys treat Third World women as sex objects is shallow and disgusting."

The first thing you have to do to translate it into Postmodenese is to make the sentence stop making sense. You do this by substituting mysterious Postmodern buzzwords or phrases for ordinary words that do make sense. For instance "white guys" can profitably be replaced by the phrase "phallocratic and panoptic (in the Foucaultian sense) Dead-White-Male subject-positions." This is because, in Postmodernese, guys no longer exist. They have become "subject-positions." The same goes for women. Therefore the phrase "Third World women" needs to be gussified up to "postcolonial female subject-positions." The phrase "the way" could properly be rendered as "the hegemonic (mis)representation and de/valorization of." As you can see, Postmodernese relies upon using as many slashes and hyphens and parentheses and whatever other kinds of marks your computer can make as possible. Thus the word "shallow" should correctly be rendered as "a textually (re)inscribed praxis of pre-disseminated, (counter)subversive 'depthlessness.'"

To be perfectly correct, your final translation should sound something like this: "The hegemonic (mis)representation and de/valorization of the always-already multi-(de)/gendered plurivocalities and (de)centered de/constructed and dialogically problematized ludic simulacra of absent/present postcolonial female subject-positions, by hyper-eroticized and orientalized phallocratic and panoptic (in the Foucaultian sense) Dead-White-Male subject-position discourse, is a textually (re)inscribed praxis of pre-disseminated, (counter)subversive depthlessness.

Q What!!??

A And if anyone asks you what all that means, you just behold them with a gaze of infinite bewilderment. Then you look them in the eye, compassionately, and tell them that the plurivocal ambiguities of (non)meaning inherent in their question obviously subvert the possibility of your delivering to them the kind of cheap and low-down phallocratic, and logocentric patriarchal hog-wallow of an answer which they are capable of understanding.

Q Well I'm not so sure I understand what Postmodernism is. And is it POSTmodernISM, postMODERNism, PoStmOdErNism, post-modernism or Postmodernism?

A It has been written in all those ways. Postmodernism—as the "post" preface implies, is something that follows modernism. However, people who think about such things as Postmodernism don't agree whether Postmodernism is a break from modernism or a continuation of modernism—or both. In fact, they don't even agree as to what modernism is, much less Postmodernism.

What Is Modernism?

Q Well, what is modernism?

A Modernism is a blanket term for an explosion of new styles and trends in the arts in the first half of the 20th century. If the modern era had a central image—it was that of a kind of non-image—a Void—and if the era had a quotation that summed it all up, it was Irish poet William Butler Yeats's lines:

Things fall apart; the centre cannot hold; Mere anarchy is loosed upon the world.

Q But what things fell apart in the modern era? What center could not hold?

A What fell apart in the modern era were the values of the 18th century, the Age of Enlightenment, also known as the Age of Reason. Probably the main value of the age, besides reason, was the idea of progress.

In the 18th century thinkers became optimistic that by using the universal values of *science, reason and logic*, they could get rid of all the myths and holy ideas that kept humanity from progressing. They felt this would eventually free humanity from misery, religion, superstition, all irrational behavior, and unfounded belief. Humanity would thus progress to a state of freedom, happiness and progress.

Francis Bacon saw progress taking the form of a wise, ethical and science-minded elite who would be the guardians of knowledge and who, though living outside the community, would nevertheless influence it. **Marx** also believed in progress, and envisioned a Utopia. But Marx's Utopian vision was of a perect world brought about by a materialist science.

Other thinkers, however, were not so optimistic. **Edmund Burke** was disgusted with the excesses of the French Revolution. And the **Marquis de Sade,** the great-granddaddy of S/M, explored the perversities of sexual freedom—painting a dark picture of human liberation. The sociologist **Max Weber** prophesied that the future would be an iron prison of reason and bureaucracy.

Q Well, maybe Yeats and all the skeptics were right. It looks as if things did fall apart. What did Science, Reason and Progress get us, after all? The 20th century has been nothing if not a dark, Kafkaesque nightmare of rationally administered death camps, death squads, Auschwitz, World Wars I and II, Hiroshima, Nagasaki, ecological disaster—and various systems of totalitarianism. And all in the name of the Enlightenment values of Science, Reason, Liberation, Freedom and Progress!

A But I haven't even told you about the biggest skeptic of all—the German philosopher **Friedrich Nietzsche**. Nietzsche had no tolerance for Enlightenment values. Reason? Universality? Morality? Progress? All these Enlightenment pretenses meant nothing to him.

He saw the world as the dance of the destructively creative and creatively destructive god Dionysus—the dance of the Will to Power—and Dionysus was his model of how to act in the chaotic storm of life. Any man who acted in such a way would be a Superman.

And Nietzsche hit the nail right on the head. After all, many 20th-century Supermen have proven that you have to destroy in order to create: Hitler, Mao,

SNAP!

Stalin, etc. Nietzsche also proclaimed the "Death of God" as well as the death of Christian morality and metaphysics. With one wave of his philosophical wand, the central symbols, institutions and beliefs of Western culture, which had already suffered a tremendous blow by the Age of Reason, disappeared—**POOF**— like a magician's rabbit into the dark folds of a cloak.

What remained were only dark waves of Nothingness—a Void.

Nature, however, abhors a vacuum, and we Westerners, unlike Buddhists and Taoists, do not tolerate voids very well. We do not drill holes in the walls of our houses and hallow these hollows, worshipping them earnestly with the words "O my Holy Hole, save me!!!"

No. We live in a culture that esteems presence over absence, icon over non-existence, voluptuous virgin over vacant vacuum, wholes over holes! And yet, where we previously had a center—whether in Christian religion or in the ideals of science and progress —suddenly we had nothing.

IS NOTHING SACRED?

Some modernists, such as Hemingway, created works of art that expressed a kind of passive recognition of this lack of a center. In his short story **"A Clean, Well-lighted Place,"** one of his characters, a waiter, reworks the Lord's Prayer and the Hail Mary—substituting "nada" (or "nothing" in Spanish) at significant places:

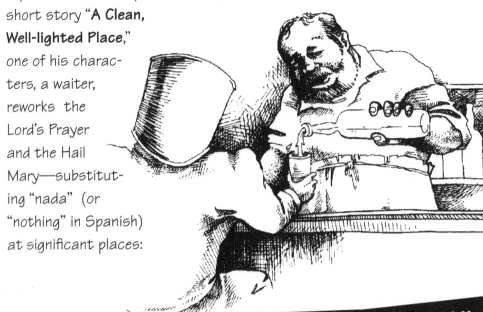

"our nada who art in nada, nada be thy name thy kingdom nada thy will be nada in nada as it is in nada. Give us this nada our daily nada and nada us our nada as we nada our nadas and nada us not into nada but deliver us from nada; pues nada. Hail nothing full of nothing, nothing is with thee..."

(SSEH 379–83)

If modern thinkers could no longer believe in a Christian God, Christian morality, or scientific progress—if there was no longer a center to Western culture—it was necessary to find a new one for, after all, we don't like voids. And it was Nietzsche—who had proclaimed the death of Enlightenment values, God and Christian morality—that showed the way. Although he had deprived Western culture of a center, he only did so by putting something else in its place—not only the idea of a Superman who is beyond good and evil but also art beyond good and evil. Thus, among all the fragmentation and chaos, amidst everything falling apart, modern artists began to look for some eternal value that was beyond all the chaos.

These artists adopted the heroic, almost Superhuman role of rediscovering the essence of humanity, of finding an eternal value beyond all the chaos, of filling in the post-Nietzschean Void in various ways. In a world without a center, aesthetics—art—became central. Art for art's sake! Modern painting was about painting—self-absorbed, self-possessed, exploring its own primary possibilities: all possible interactions between perception, memory, identity.

Bohemian, avant-garde, experimenting with traditional genres and styles—modern artists, who brought modern art to its fullest blossoming sometime between 1910 and the 1930s, rallied around poet Ezra Pound's battle cry "Make it new," seeing themselves as creators of the new rather than as preservers of old cultural forms.

MAKE It NEW

Such art became a way to represent the eternal in the midst of chaos. Cubism drew inspiration from the simple geometries of African sculpture, dematerialized objects, breaking them down into their basic geometric forms. Cubist artists painted, as Picasso put it, "not what you see, but what you know is there."

Impressionists such as Manet and Monet broke up objects in a different way, painting with dabs of color rather than continuous brush strokes, so as to suggest the play of light over the surfaces of objects. Thus objects in the Impressionist world were not solid, but appeared to have decomposed into fragments of light.

In literature, looking for an inner truth beyond appearances, writers such as D.H. Lawrence, T.S. Eliot, James Joyce and William But-ler Yeats attempted to create a new center by drawing upon exotic myths made known to them through recent discoveries in anthropology and the translations of the texts of Eastern religions and tribal myths.

Yeats wrote down his vision of vast, historical cycles of time turning and turning in ever widening spirals. He saw that the center could not hold, so he populated it with heroes, damsels and fairies from Celtic myth and folklore. D. H. Lawrence, in his novels and short-stories filled the post-Nietzschean Void with "primitive" gods, goddesses and energies: the Sexuality of the Virgin and the Gypsy, the Sun, the Snake, the Dark-Skinned Native. These images drew upon the findings of Sigmund Freud, depicting a conscious mind haunted and split by primitive, dark, erotic, violent subconscious urges and drives. James Joyce's A Portrait of the Artist as a Young Man, the story of a sensitive youth seeking to escape the confines of his Catholic upbringing in Dublin, is based on the ancient Greek myth of the hero Daedelus attempting to escape the Labyrinth. Thus, it has a myth at its center.

One symbol that attempted to fill in the Void that had been left by the "death of God" was the symbol of the machine. Poet Ezra Pound saw words as machines. The poet William Carlos Williams said that the whole poem is a machine made up of words. Modern architects thought of houses as machines for living in. In fact, all of society was becoming more machine-like: bureaucratic, technical, rational. From this kind of machine-like efficiency arose war machines as powerful as they were efficient: In Italy, the war machine of the Superman Mussolini. In Germany, Superman Hitler's Nazi trains ran on time, delivering their human cargo to death camps like Auschwitz and Buchenwald. These camps themselves drew upon modernist planning and architectural principles. And the Nazi war machine had its own center—the myth of the Super Race—the superiority of blue-eyed, blond members of the Aryan race.

So one problem with modernism is that science and reason didn't just create progress—they created Auschwitz and Hiroshima. And there were other problems—artistic ones.

Modern art and literature became increasingly difficult to understand.

Modernism - became High modernism. High modernism peaked in 1922, with the publication of James Joyce's **Ulysses** and

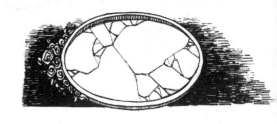

T.S. Eliot's "**The Wasteland**."

In both **Ulysses** and **Finnegan's Wake**, Joyce experimented with a stream-of-consciousness style, plunging the reader within the fluid, shifting free-flow of his characters' psyches.

Eliot's "**Wasteland**" experimented with a fragmented poetry full of literary, historical and mythological tidbits from around the world—depicting a soul and a society in fragmentation and despair, seeking reintegration, a new center. Both Joyce and Eliot rejected the straightforward, and rational flow of the story or theme. They also rejected traditional character development, favoring instead a fragmented style. But this dislike of conventional character development and the celebration instead, of private, subjective experience added to the tendency of modernism's artists, assembled in small groups in Paris, Berlin, Rome, Vienna, London, New York, Chicago, Copenhagen, Munich or Moscow, to view themselves as an exiled, alienated cultural elite.

In "**The Metamorphosis**" the writer Franz Kafka symbolized this alienation of the artist with the image of a huge human-sized bug trapped in an absurd human environment. Such artists created works so challenging and weird that they could only be appreciated by a narrow audience. This only further added to their elitist image.

Modern art, in fact, was so far-out that it divided culture into "Highbrow" and "Lowbrow." It excluded the middle class, who could not understand it, and gave rise to a kind of "priesthood" of scholars and critics. Their job was and is to explain modernism's mysteries. To read James Joyce's **Ulysses**, T.S. Eliot's "**Wasteland**" or Ezra Pound's "**Cantos**" is an adventure. You need a guide, as though you were exploring the Amazon.

What Is Postmodernism?

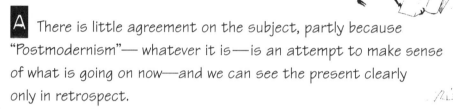

Q **Then how does Postmodernism differ from modernism?**

A There is little agreement on the subject, partly because "Postmodernism"— whatever it is—is an attempt to make sense of what is going on now—and we can see the present clearly only in retrospect.

IHAB HASSAN

One Postmodern theorist, Ihab Hassan, offers a table of differences between the two movements:

Modernism		Postmodernism
Form (conjunctive/closed)	◄·············►	Antiform (disjunctive/open)
Purpose	◄·············►	Play
Design	◄·············►	Chance
Hierarchy	◄·············►	Anarchy
Art Object/Finished Work	◄·············►	Process/Performance/ Happening
Presence	◄·············►	Absence
Centering	◄·············►	Dispersal
Genre/Boundary	◄·············►	Text/Intertext
Root/Depth	◄·············►	Rhizome/Surface

(TPL 267–8)

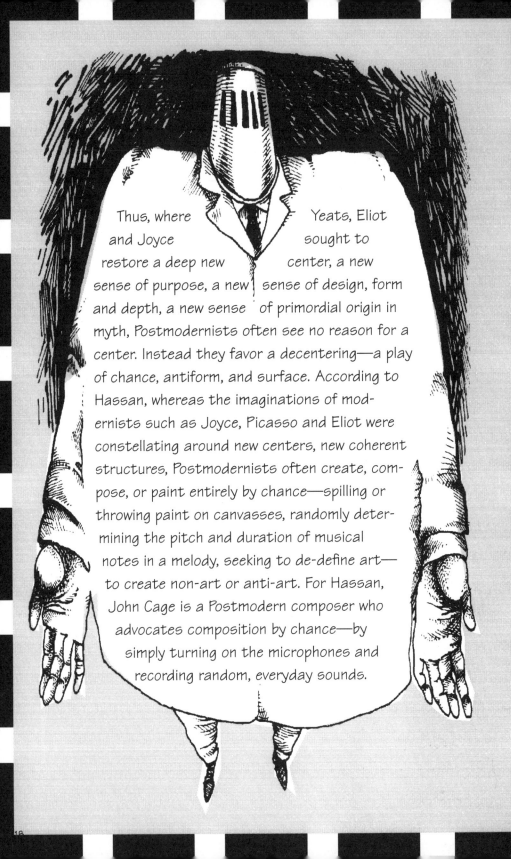

Thus, where Yeats, Eliot and Joyce sought to restore a deep new center, a new sense of purpose, a new sense of design, form and depth, a new sense of primordial origin in myth, Postmodernists often see no reason for a center. Instead they favor a decentering—a play of chance, antiform, and surface. According to Hassan, whereas the imaginations of modernists such as Joyce, Picasso and Eliot were constellating around new centers, new coherent structures, Postmodernists often create, compose, or paint entirely by chance—spilling or throwing paint on canvasses, randomly determining the pitch and duration of musical notes in a melody, seeking to de-define art—to create non-art or anti-art. For Hassan, John Cage is a Postmodern composer who advocates composition by chance—by simply turning on the microphones and recording random, everyday sounds.

Q It all sounds pretty chaotic. It's no wonder that we need "map-makers," intellectuals to chart the depthless new world without a center. Who are some of these "map-makers"?

THE MAP-MAKERS
Important Postmodern Thinkers
Jean-Francois Lyotard

A Jean-Francois Lyotard was born in France in 1924 and taught in Algeria, Brazil and California, before becoming professor of philosophy at the University of Paris in 1968. In 1985 he became director of the College International de Philosophie.

For some 15 years he was associated with a leftist group called **Socialism or Barbarism**, which, among other things, criticized Soviet-style communism. Although Lyotard became disillusioned with socialism and Marxism as early as 1964, the events of the student revolt in Paris, in May of 1968, confirmed his unrest.

Discourse, figure

In 1971 we find him beginning a long, post-Marxist period in which he is given to thinking about philosophy, language and the arts. His book *Discourse, figure*, argues with the concept put forth by Jacques Lacan that the unconscious mind is like a language. Instead, Lyotard suggests that the unconscious is not so much like a language as it is visual and figural, like the figures one draws or paints. Language, after all, is flat, two dimensional. It represses desire. Dreams, on the other hand, are visual, figural, alive with three-dimensional dream figures, and dripping with desire. Like much modern painting, dreams are fragmented. In their attempt to make unconscious material visual, dreams disrupt the kind of linear awareness that language requires. The visual, figure-making nature of the unconscious, though at work within language, disrupts language, disrupts the rational order of language. This is because the figural nature of the unconscious is difficult to represent in language.

The figural resists representation in the same sense that the Holocaust resists representation. At Auschwitz the Nazis would drown out the screams of the victims in the death camps by playing music loudly. Similarly, to attempt to represent Auschwitz in language—to reduce the degradation, death and stench to a concept—drowns out the screams. According to Lyotard, it is therefore necessary that the Holocaust remains immemorial—that it remains being that which cannot be remembered—but also that which cannot be forgotten. Thus, any art attempting to represent the Holocaust should continue to haunt us with its inability to represent the unrepresentable, to say the unsayable. It should continue to haunt us with the feeling that there is something Other than representation.

Lyotard offers the example of Masaccio's **Trinity**, painted on the walls of Santa Maria Novella, in Florence, which displays both medieval and Renaissance elements. By attempting to present two impossibly different eras, the painting seems to say that there is always an Other which cannot be truly represented.

Another example Lyotard offers is Cezanne's **Mont Saint-Victoire**—a simultaneous attempt to present two different modes of vision: vision with a distinct focal center and vision which is peripheral, diffuse, indistinct. Again, two heterogeneous elements.

Q **Heterogeneous?**

A Yes. Heterogeneous means "made up of dissimilar elements."

Poetic metaphor accomplishes the same. When I say "my love is a rose" I am invoking a heterogeneous difference. After all, a rose and my love may have very little in common.

Because all these works of art bring our attention to the Other, to a radical difference, they are political.

The Postmodern Condition

In 1974, the year Postmodern novelist Thomas Pynchon's **Gravity's Rainbow**, won the National Book Award, "streaking" became a fad in the United States, Mama Cass of the Mamas and the Papas choked to death on a sandwich, and a Soviet probe touched down on Mars, Lyotard gained international fame for **The Postmodern Condition: a report on knowledge,** an account commissioned by the Council of Universities of the Quebec government. The report surveys the status of science and technology, and has become something of a bible of Postmodernism.

Lyotard argues that for the past few decades science has increasingly investigated language, linguistic theories, communications, cybernetics, informatics, computers and computer languages, information storage, data banks, and problems of translation from one computer language to another. He proclaimed that these technological changes would have a major impact on knowledge.

Thus, in 1974 he predicted that no knowledge will survive that cannot be

and storage of information will no longer depend on individuals, but on computers. Information will be produced and sold. Nations will fight for information the way they used to fight for territory. Information will zip around the globe at the speed of electricity, and people will try to steal it. The role of the state will grow weaker. Taking the place of states, huge, multinational corporations will dominate.

But having said all this about the direction of scientific knowledge, Lyotard adds that scientific knowledge is not the only kind of knowledge. His interest, it turns out, is not so much in scientific knowledge and the scientific method, per se, but in how scientific knowledge and method legitimize themselves—how they make themselves believable and trustworthy. And at this point Lyotard makes a distinction between scientific talk and narrative talk. Of course he doesn't use the word "talk." He uses scientific "discourse" and narrative "discourse."

translated into computer language—into quantities of information. Learning will no longer be associated with the training of minds—with teachers training students. For the transmission

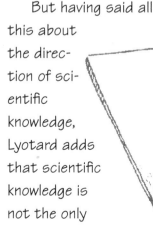

A Yes. I will give you some examples that Lyotard does not use, but which help explain his theory. When members of the Winnebago tribe sit around a fire and hear a chant of how the world was created by thought, or the Boshon-go, a Bantu tribe, chant how the god Bumba vomited forth the Moon and Stars, or when the early Japanese heard a chant about the formation of Heaven and Earth from a Primordial Egg—they are listen-ing to narrative, to popular sto-ries, myths, legends and tales.

And such myths legitimize themselves—make themselves believable—just in the telling. And at the same time they legitimize the society in which they are told. The teller of the myth does not have to argue or prove, like a sci-entist, when he chants the story of Bumba vomiting the Moon and the Stars. Merely in performing the myth, in the vibrations of the chant, the beat, the rhythm—the sense of natural time is dissolved and the awareness opens to mythic time: to narrative time. According to Lyotard, nursery rhymes and some repetitive forms of contemporary music attempt to enter the same space of myth-ic time.

The chanter of the myth legit-imizes it simply by stating:

"Here is the myth of Bumba, Vomiting the Moon and Stars, as I've always heard it chanted. I will chant it to you in my turn. Listen."

He then chants the myth. When he is finished he says:

"Here ends the myth of Bumba. The man who has chanted it to you is Pongo."

The narrator has authority to chant the chant because he has heard it chanted himself. Anyone listening gains the same authority merely by listening. It is even claimed that the chant has been chanted forever, that Bumba Himself was the first one to chant the chant. The myth, the chanter, the audience, all form a kind of social bond—a social group that legitimizes itself through the chanting of the myth. The myth requires no authorization or legitimization other than itself. The myth defines what has the right to be said and done in the culture.

But according to Lyotard, scientific discourse is a different kind of language game than narrative discourse—than myth. Scientific discourse cannot legitimize itself.

Q Language game?

A Here Lyotard is drawing upon the work of the philosopher Ludwig Wittgenstein. In his early work Wittgenstein looked for the perfect, logical language that could state everything with clarity and precision. Any other use of language—such as telling a joke, reciting poetry, or chanting the myth of Bumba—he would have seen as meaningless.

But then he changed his mind. He began to see that there are many different language games that we play. For instance—praying, singing, telling jokes, gossiping, swearing, making a promise, taking a vow, pronouncing a couple man and wife, telling a lie. Science is a different kind of language game from that of myth. It cannot legitimize itself or validate itself by its own procedures. In the language game of science the scientist makes denotative statements rather than mythical ones.

Q Denotative statements?

A A denotative statement is one such as "'Moon' is a term that denotes a material body (satellite) which rotates and orbits around the planet Earth with a uniform and known speed and at a definite distance, according to known Newtonian (or Einsteinian) laws."

In the language game of science "Moon" does not refer to something that, along with the Stars, was, at the opening of creation, vomited forth by Bumba. The scientist, unlike the chanter of the myth of Bumba, must be able to **prove** his denotative statements about the Moon and **disprove** any opposing or contradictory statements about the Moon. [*In the 19th century, this was known as the rule of verification. In the 20th century, this is called the rule of falsification.*]

Scientific discourse and narrative are different language games, and what counts as a good move in one game does not count as a good move in the other. You cannot prove narrative, mythic, knowledge on the basis of science.

And what science cannot do is to legitimize its own activity. It cannot answer questions such as: Why should there be scientific activity in the first place? Or: Why should society encourage and support scientific research?

According to Lyotard, **since science cannot depend upon science to legitimize itself, it must turn to narrative!**

Q Do you mean to say that NASA scientists, in order to legitimize the moon-shot, chant the myth of how Bumba vomited the Moon?

A No. According to Lyotard, science has depended upon two other narratives. The first is political, the second, philosophical.

The first narrative science relies upon in order to legitimize itself is because the great thinkers of the era, men such as

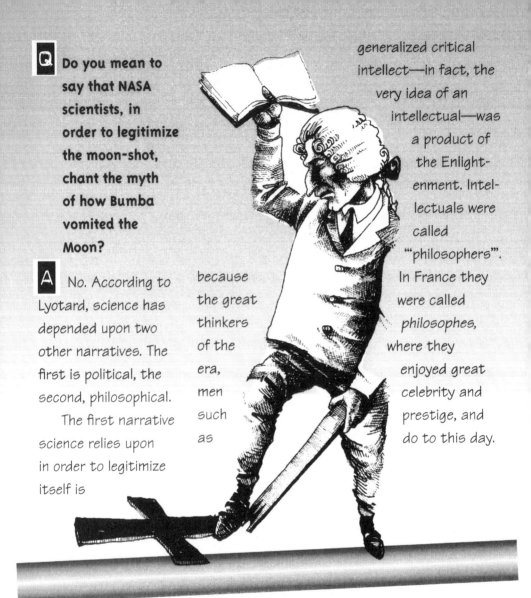

generalized critical intellect—in fact, the very idea of an intellectual—was a product of the Enlightenment. Intellectuals were called "'philosophers'". In France they were called philosophes, where they enjoyed great celebrity and prestige, and do to this day.

associated with the 18th century, the Enlightenment and the French Revolution. The 18th century was also called the Age of Reason,—in France Le Siècle des Lumières—

Voltaire, Rousseau, Buffon, Condillac and Diderot, applied **reason** to every area of life: religion, morality, politics, social life.

The idea of a place in society for a kind of

Reject religious authority! Down with old things like metaphysics, ignorance, superstition, intolerance and parochialism! Let the rational faculties of the mind,

wedded to science, advance knowledge to ever expanding vistas! Let reason unlock the laws of nature and usher in an optimistic age! Let the practical discoveries of science allow men and women to get on with the proper business of seeking happiness! And happiness means political freedom! Let the happiness of humanity on earth mean the liberty—the liberation of humanity! All this means progress! Let science and reason bring progress and freedom!

Joined to this French political narrative of freedom is a German narrative: Hegel's philosophy of the Unity of all Knowledge. For Hegel, knowledge played an essential part in the gradual evolution of the human mind from ignorance to total being.

Both the French Enlightenment narrative and the German knowledge narrative are what Lyotard calls **metanarratives** or **grand narratives,** big stories, stories of mythic proportions— that claim to be able to account for, explain and subordinate all lesser, little, local narratives. Some other metanarratives are the philosophies of Marxism or the narrative of Christian salvation. Thus the narrative of a successful Mars expedition in which a 3" x 3" nano-rover lands on the

-110 Celsius surface of the planet to generate and transmit back to Earth digital images of the Mars-scape,— is a little narrative that is part of the big story—the metanarrative—of the freedom, the liberation of humanity (French), and the attainment of a pure, self-conscious spirit—the Unity of all Knowledge (German).

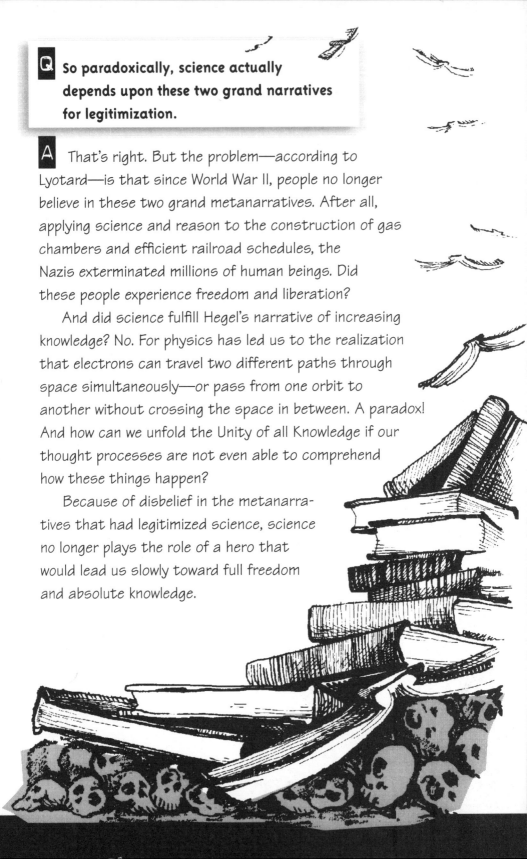

Q So paradoxically, science actually depends upon these two grand narratives for legitimization.

A That's right. But the problem—according to Lyotard—is that since World War II, people no longer believe in these two grand metanarratives. After all, applying science and reason to the construction of gas chambers and efficient railroad schedules, the Nazis exterminated millions of human beings. Did these people experience freedom and liberation?

And did science fulfill Hegel's narrative of increasing knowledge? No. For physics has led us to the realization that electrons can travel two different paths through space simultaneously—or pass from one orbit to another without crossing the space in between. A paradox! And how can we unfold the Unity of all Knowledge if our thought processes are not even able to comprehend how these things happen?

Because of disbelief in the metanarratives that had legitimized science, science no longer plays the role of a hero that would lead us slowly toward full freedom and absolute knowledge.

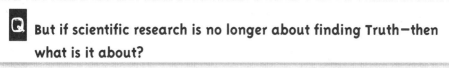
A When science encounters paradoxes, such as the electron that goes opposite directions simultaneously, it abandons its search for decidable truths and seeks to legitimize itself through **performativity**. Science stops asking, What kind of research will unfold the laws of nature?" and begins asking, What kind of research will work best? And to "work best" means What kind of research can generate more of the same kind of research? Can it perform? Can it produce more of the same kind of research? So science is no longer concerned with truth but with performativity—performing—producing more of the same kind of research because the more research you produce, the more proof you produce and the more you are seen as being right, and the more money and power you get.

So when people no longer believe in the metanarratives that legitimize science, science is then forced to legitimize itself—just as the myth of Bumba vomiting the Moon and Stars legitimizes itself by itself. Both science and people chanting the Bumba chant can then say,

"We do what we do, because that's the way we do it."

Q Then what's the difference between the two, after all?

A The difference, for Lyotard, is that where traditional societies are under the spell of one dominant narrative, such as the myth of Bumba, Postmodern society is a society in which no one narrative—big or little—no one language game dominates. In Postmodern societies many micronarratives are jammed together. And this carnival of narratives replaces the monolithic presence of one metanarrative.

Q But doesn't this mean the disappearance of our universal system of meaning? Doesn't this just create a void?

A Yes. But this void is filled in by swirling galaxies of little stories—little micronarratives. The void is filled in by a kind of storytelling that does not seek to legitimize itself through reference to a single grand narrative outside itself. For instance, a teller of tales in ancient India, sitting under his banyan tree, would have told thousands of stories—but all these stories would have been legitimized by the grand Hindu narrative of the liberation of the human soul through Enlightenment.

In contrast, the story-teller at your local bookstore, or visiting the children at your local school, may tell a traditional Eskimo or Native American Trickster tale, or the story of Rapunzel letting down her long, golden hair for a handsome young prince, or the story of Bumba vomiting the

Moon and Stars—and tell them all in one sitting. None of these stories seeks legitimization or proof through some grand narrative. Each story, while it is being told, is its own proof, and the proof of all the others. It is legitimized simply by doing what it does.

Like the Postmodern storyteller's grab bag of stories, Postmodern society is made up of zillions of incompatible little stories—micronarratives. And not one of these little stories can dominate or explain the rest.

Q **But isn't Lyotard's story about disbelief in metanarratives just another metanarrative? Isn't he being authoritarian about how there can be no authorities?**

A Yes. Lyotard has been attacked on those grounds. In fact, his notion that people have stopped believing in grand narratives because such narratives marginalize minorities assumes that people universally believe in justice. And that is a metanarrative.

Yet, despite its inadequacies, Lyotard's definition of Postmodernism as **incredulity toward metanarratives** continues to have great influence.

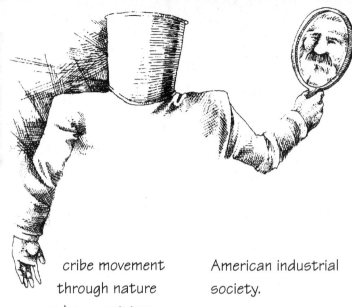

Fredric Jameson

A second influential Postmodern thinker is Fredric Jameson. As a Marxist, Jameson is interested in the relationship of the individual to the world of objects, whether those objects be cans of soup or multinational corporations. Like most Marxists, his reflections on this relationship always lead back to historical reality.

For instance, Hemingway's prose style—his bare, pared-down sentences—can describe movement through nature and suggest tension and resentment between his macho characters. The skill of a bullfighter or trout fisherman in Hemingway reflects the American admiration of technical skill—but rejects the way in which industrial society alienates people. Thus skill is displayed in leisure activities, far from industry, usually by expatriates who have alienated themselves from American industrial society.

"Postmodernism, or the Cultural Logic of Late Capitalism"

Lyotard *celebrates* the multiple, incompatible, heterogeneous, fragmented, contradictory and ambivalent nature of Postmodern society while Jameson distrusts and dislikes it. In his famous essay "Postmodernism: or the Cultural Logic of Late Capitalism," Jameson does not see the

Postmodern era as postindustrial—as an ebb in the tide of capitalism. Rather, he sees it as an intensification and latest phase of a capitalist world system.

Jameson was heavily influenced by Ernest Mandel's

Late Capitalism, which broke down the 19th and 20th centuries into definite historical periods.

FIRST: from 1700 to 1850, the period of market capitalism. During this era industrial capital accumulated mostly in national markets.

SECOND: monopoly capitalism, during the age of imperialism. National markets expanded into world markets. Though these markets were based in particular imperial nation-states, they depended upon outlying areas for raw materials and cheap labor.

THIRD—the Postmodern
phase erupted on the world scene with
the unrestricted growth of multinational corporations—such as Coca-Cola. This is the
purest form of capitalism yet to emerge—
invading nature by destroying the pre-capitalist
forms of agriculture—and invading the unconscious mind by advertising.

Mandell's history inspired Jameson to proclaim
three cultural periods—in each of which a unique
cultural logic dominates:

The era of the bourgeoisie, historical novel.

Jameson admires modernism because modernist culture
expressed its dissatisfaction with the world. Take Edvard
Munch's painting *The Scream*. For Jameson it is a desperate cry
expressing the great modernist themes of alienation, root-
lessness, lack of identity, solitude, and social fragmentation.

Similarly, Van Gogh's painting *Peasant Shoes* criticizes an entire world of peasant poverty and misery. Modernist buildings,
such as Le Corbusier's "great pilotis" stand out as grand utopian beacons in bright contrast to the degraded city surrounding
them. They express a politically passionate vision of Utopia.

But then the curtain opens on the third age—

Postmodern cultural forms reflect the dislocation and
fragmentation of language communities—splintered

into small groups—each speaking "a curious private language of its own, each profession developing its private code or dialect, and finally each individual coming to be a kind of linguistic island, separated from everyone else" (PCS 114).

Thus, according to Jameson, Postmodern city-dwellers are alienated, living in an hallucination, an exhilarating blur, a reality evaporating into mere images, spectacles, strange new warps in time and space, fixated on commodities, on products, on images, like the explosion of Andy Warhol's pop art, on flows of images stolen from consumer culture and reproduced with industrial repetition, Campbell's Soup cans, Brillo boxes, bottles of Coca-Cola, collages of identical images of Hollywood stars such as Marilyn Monroe, all sameness, all surface—all depthlessness. Compared to Van Gogh's **Peasant Shoes**, which expresses a real world of rural misery, Warhol's **Diamond Dust Shoes** expresses a depthless-

ness with no link to any reality: the collapse of the distinction between high culture and low culture; masses of spectators abandoned to a gaze of image addiction; TV images stripped of reality, leaving only a surface, a simulacrum, schlock, kitsch, B movies, pulp fiction, advertising, motels, Readers Digest culture; the merely decorative, superficial, gratuitous eclecticism of Postmodern architecture cannibalizing all the architectural styles of the past, the Bonaventure Hotel in Los Angeles a monument of Postmodern architectural space.

But wait! Jameson can't get into the hotel! The entrance is concealed! But then he finds the entrance! It looks something like a back door! He enters a Postmodern hyperspace! He rides elevators and escalators eternally floating up and down like giant gondolas. He views the closed cylindrical towers! He feels dizzy, drowning in a bewildering emptiness. He wants a map so that he can map his way to the external world!

Jameson feels that his dizziness when faced with Postmodern culture is similar to our incapacity to map our relationship to the centerless world of vast computer networks and multinational corporations. Postmodern theory, too, offers no map, being more a **symptom** of the centerless Postmodern world than a **cure**.

Jameson is perhaps most well known for his distinction between parody and pastiche. One thing that Postmodernity has exploded is the subject—the ego. In the age of modernity we still believed in the subject—the ego. Artists such as Hemingway possessed a unified ego and identity—even if it was an alienated one. And possessing an identity, they possessed a style that could be the subject of parody—you could make fun of it by imitating it. Every year, for instance, there is a literary contest in which writers imitate Hemingway's style in a humorous way.

Every year we met at Harry's bar. We drank there. And every year was a good year. And we sat and drank and imitated Hemingway's style. And we were good there.

But Postmodernity has fragmented language and the subject—both have become schizoid. Jameson feels that parody and satire are only possible in an era of healthy linguistic normality.

Q **You mean like in Gulliver's Travels, Jonathan Swift was able to satirize the abnormal language of scientific reason because everyone knew what normal speech was like?**

A Yes. But in the Postmodern age, there is no linguistic normality. Thus we can only produce **pastiche**—like an impersonator who randomly starts out impersonating Bogart, and then switches, in the middle of his line, to Marilyn Monroe, and then to Boy George or James Dean, and then to Ronald Reagan. In pastiche there is only this smorgasbord of quotations—like a dozen different movie and MTV videos and television shows spliced randomly together.

As a Marxist who believes that the world is run by historical forces, Jameson's biggest gripe about the Postmodern era is that it signals the end of a genuine awareness of history. But Jameson feels that an awareness of history is precisely what we now need to piece together our fragmented Postmodern language and selves, which, like Humpty Dumpty, have become fragmented. It is what we need to unify the past-present-future of the sentence—to unify our psyches and our lives.

What we need is what Jameson calls an **"aesthetic of cognitive mapping"** to represent our imaginary relationship to reality. What we need, according to Jameson, is Marxism—a science that can tell what is imaginary and what is real—that can recover true historical consciousness and normalcy.

Q **But wouldn't Lyotard say that Marxism is a metanarrative?**

A Yes. And so you can see that not all Postmodernists agree. In fact, Jameson seems overcome by the flow of images in the Postmodern media—but our next "map-maker," Jean Baudrillard, seems to suggest a kind of passive surrender to this flow.

Jean Baudrillard
and the Death of the Real

You are wired. The passive victim of TV, computer, and advertising. You are hypnotized by the tube, by the obscene flow of images. You raise your eyelids. A vampiress is kneeling over you—voluptuously—the muscles of her neck, the ivory curve of her shoulders, illumined as if by cool moonlight. She licks her scarlet lips like an animal, glazing them with a sheen of moisture, her engorged tongue glistening as it laps the white teeth. She leans closer, you feel her cool breath, then the sharpness of incisors penetrating your neck. You close your eyes in a languorous ecstasy and wait—wait with beating heart.

This, according to the imagery of Postmodern theorist Jean Baudrillard, is similar to society's relationship to the world of mass media, advertising, television, newspapers, magazines. The era of mass communications invades our darkened rooms, embracing us with its cool, lunar light, penetrating into our most private recesses. We succumb to the fatal attraction, surrendering ourselves in an ecstasy of communication.

The thought of Jean Baudrillard is part of a **New Wave of French theory** that broke on American shores in the '70s '80s and '90s—replacing the frenzy over former waves dominated by post- World War II figures such as Sartre. Just as Nietzsche once proclaimed the Death of God, Baudrillard's thought declares the **death of modernity, the death of the real**, and **the death of sex**. Baudrillard undermines deep foundations of thought in disciplines such as Marxism, semiotics, political science, economics, religious studies, anthropology, literature, film and media studies—to name just a few.

In May of 1968—while miniskirt-clad American women were celebrating No Bra Day by burning their brassieres and other undies, while American hippies were tripping to "Purple Haze," "Mellow Yellow," and "Mrs. Robinson"—Parisian youth, backed by Communists and other Marxists, took to the streets in a defiant and jubilant mood, creating something between a carnival and a revolution. Parisian universities were eventually shut down by the student strike, and factory workers followed suit. Production and education came to a halt. Under the threat of a radical overthrow of the system, de Gaulle left the country. By June, however, it was summer vacation time, turning the would-be student revolutionaries into beachgoers. The workers, encouraged by de Gaulle, returned to their jobs—and things were soon back to normal.

Nevertheless, the mass contagion of the movement left deep impressions on some of the participants. One of these was Jean Baudrillard, who, for many years to come, would still continue to be influenced by Marxist thought, but would feel increasingly that Marxist philosophy is insufficient to explain life in late capitalist societies. So he began looking also to structuralism and semiotics to supplement Marxism.

A HORSE IS A HORSE, OF COURSE, OF COURSE.

Q Structuralism? Semiotics?

A Yes. At the same time as the student uprising, revolutionary events were taking place in the study of language and culture as well. The Swiss linguist Ferdinand de Saussure argued that meaning in language is not produced by a collection of sounds corresponding to concepts and things.

According to Saussure, there is no natural correspondence between the "sound" horse, the concept "horse" and a horse. Rather, he theorized, language is a system of differences, something like the red, yellow and green lights in a traffic signal.

43

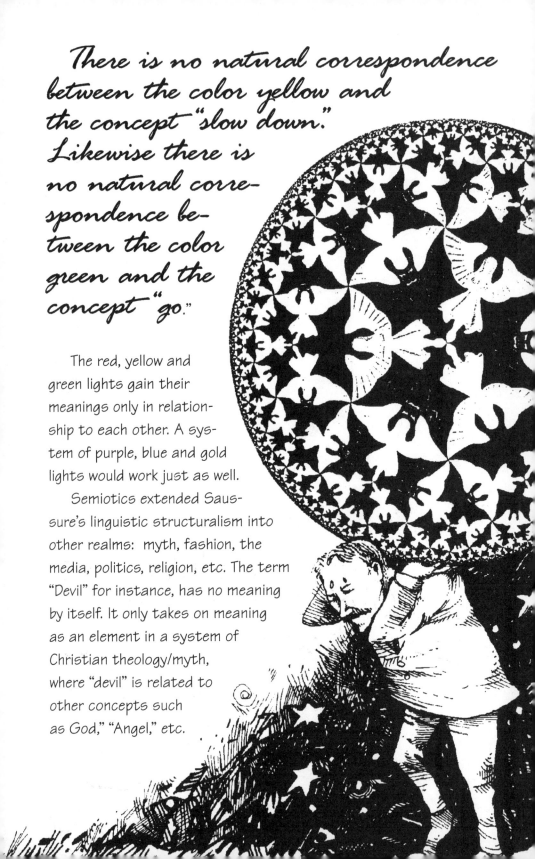

There is no natural correspondence between the color yellow and the concept "slow down." Likewise there is no natural correspondence between the color green and the concept "go."

The red, yellow and green lights gain their meanings only in relationship to each other. A system of purple, blue and gold lights would work just as well.

Semiotics extended Saussure's linguistic structuralism into other realms: myth, fashion, the media, politics, religion, etc. The term "Devil" for instance, has no meaning by itself. It only takes on meaning as an element in a system of Christian theology/myth, where "devil" is related to other concepts such as God," "Angel," etc.

Early Writings

Semiotics is the structuralist study of various systems of meaning, like myths, traffic signals, language, fashion, etc. Baudrillard's works combine a semiotic, structuralist, study of culture with a neo-Marxist analysis. For instance, in his early works—*The System of Objects, The Society of Consumption* and *For a Critique of the Political Economy of the Sign*—Baudrillard argues that just as a young boy who grows up among wolves becomes wolflike, people in Postmodern society, growing up in a world of objects—become more objectlike.

Though Postmodern society is based on the consumption of commodities—on buying and using things—this consumption can never make us happy.

Q **But don't commodities satisfy our natural needs?**

A This is not what Marx believed. For Marx, an object, before it is a commodity, has a natural **use value**. A car is useful because it is pleasurable to drive—because it lets you feel the voluptuous curvature of the earth—and because it transports you to various places.

However, Marx also believed that in a capitalist society an object becomes a commodity and takes on an **exchange value**. The car can be exchanged for money. But Baudrillard saw this Marxist assessment of an object as too limiting, and supplemented it with a **semiotic** analysis—an analysis of the meaning of the object. For, like traffic lights, commodities have meanings. In this analysis commodities don't just satisfy natural needs—rather society creates our needs. Human beings, after all, have a deep desire to distinguish themselves from other human beings through systems of social differentiation. For members of tribal cultures these differences might be signaled by the use of certain tattoos or feathers.

But in our society, when a consumer buys a Mercedes instead of a Volkswagen, for example, he is buying into a whole system of needs that is at once rational, homogeneous, systematic and hierarchical. The purchase of the Mercedes differentiates the buyer socially from people who drive Volkswagens, and this purchase helps integrate him, systematically and rationally, into a homogeneous level of society, a level of society in which everyone drives a Mercedes.

Thus, for Baudrillard, Marx did not recognize the symbolic, semiotic aspect of the object—the fact that when you buy a Mercedes it signifies something. The Mercedes, besides having a use value, serves as a sign of the consumer's prestige, rank, and social standing. Thus consumption is not just consumption but conspicuous consumption. We display what we buy, conspicuously, in order to differentiate ourselves socially.

And you can't buy just one object in order to enter a social level, you need to buy into an entire system of objects. Thus when you are picking out your Mercedes, you also need to shop for a tennis club, an estate in an exclusive neighborhood, a good private school for your children, a fashionable vacation spot, etc. A need, then, is not so much a need for a particular object as it is a need to **distinguish** oneself socially, a need for social **difference** and **meaning**.

Neither is consumption primarily for pleasure—for it requires immense resources and energy. A person must earn the money and leisure-time to obtain the Mercedes and show it off. The effort required to do this often demands the denial of pleasure. Consumption, then, is not natural—something we automatically inherit from nature—but cultural. The consumption, display and use of objects takes place on the basis of cultural codes that demand we conform

by ceaselessly buying into the latest fads and trends. These codes are just like the rules of grammar that underlie a language—making communication possible. The codes organize commodities into hierarchical systems of meaning based on price and prestige. This tiring feeding frenzy of consumption, this search for being, meaning and prestige through consumption, causes fatigue and alienation in the heroes of consumption. Always latent in consumption, then, lurks a spirit of rebellion. Consumers reach a point of refusal—they get fed up and end up burning their bras or erupting into more radical forms of social change.

"The Orders of Simulacra"

During the 1970s and 1980s Baudrillard stopped emphasizing his Marxist leanings and was heralded as the most advanced theorist of media and society in the Postmodern era.

Postmodern societies, dominated by computers and television, have moved into a new reality, which he outlines in "The Orders of Simulacra."

Q **Simulacra? [Simulacra, plural; simulacrum, singular]**

A Yes. For Baudrillard simulacra are copies of real objects or events. In "The Orders of Simulacra," he describes how the relationship between the real and the simulacrum has changed through history. During the feudal era, when Guineveres blew kisses from the ramparts of castles to Lancelots in shining armor, when the feudal lord was the symbol of earthly authority, and the Virgin Mary illumined the stained glass windows and the hearts of her devotees, society was organized by a relationship to a system of fixed signs, which were limited in number and supposedly divine.

For instance, we can read in Lancelot's coat of arms his social rank and status. The social status of the princess blowing kisses from the ramparts, is signified by her dress and by her adherence to the conventions of courtly love. And, of course, all these codes of behavior and dress are divinely sanctioned by the symbols of Mary and of Jesus shining

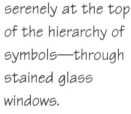

serenely at the top of the hierarchy of symbols—through stained glass windows.

In such societies one is assigned to a fixed social space, like a caste, and mobility between social classes or castes is impossible. **A serf, laboring in the fields, could not become a knight.**

Then, in the period of early modernity, from the Renaissance to the beginning of the Industrial Revolution, the rigid order of the feudal era broke down due to the rise of the bourgeoisie.

During the medieval period the world was created in the image of God. But in the era of early modernity, images, signs and symbols were not divine but artificial and proliferated in the fields of theater, fashion, art and politics as the new rising class attempted to create the world in its own image.

For Baudrillard, a symbol of this age was Camille Renault, an old cook, turned sculptor, who lived in the Ardennes and discovered the perfect substance for reproducing the world in his own image—Reinforced Concrete. From this he fashioned chairs, drawers, sewing machines, an entire orchestra, including violins, sheep, a hog, trees. According to Baudrillard, Renault ruled like a god over his perfect world made possible by concrete—which for him was like a mental substance. Stucco also emerged in this period as a medium of Baroque art, and gave rise to Baudrillard's supreme example of this age—the Stucco Angel. It was only one more step to plastic.

But simulacra molded of stucco, concrete (and later plastic), though counterfeit, produced a new world of forms made of a deathless, flexible, indestructible material. Baudrillard sees this stage of the simulacrum as the beginning stage of the simulacrum— the First Order of Simulacra.

The Second Order of Simulacra appears with the advent of the Industrial Revolution. The simulacra now become infinitely reproducible through industrial mass production. Whereas Camille Renault molded his artificial world by hand, in the industrial era mechanized means of mass assembly and production enable a Renault automobile factory to turn out masses of exact replicas of cars.

When photography and cinema arrive on the scene, even **art** succumbs to the force of mechanical reproduction. Reproduction is governed by market forces, which now become the dominant principle—replacing the world of natural objects.

But, according to Baudrillard, we are now in the Third Order of Simulacra—the era of Postmodernity—the era of **models**. No longer is the simulacrum a counterfeit like Camille Renault's concrete hog, or an infinite series, like automobiles rolling off the assembly line—but

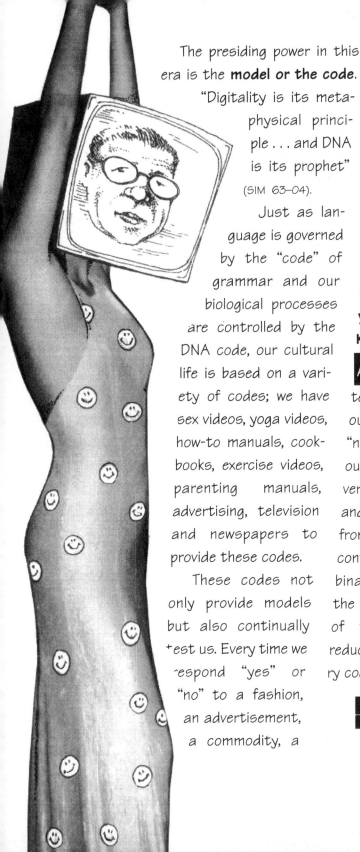

The presiding power in this era is the **model or the code**. "Digitality is its metaphysical principle . . . and DNA is its prophet" (SIM 63–04).

Just as language is governed by the "code" of grammar and our biological processes are controlled by the DNA code, our cultural life is based on a variety of codes; we have sex videos, yoga videos, how-to manuals, cookbooks, exercise videos, parenting manuals, advertising, television and newspapers to provide these codes.

These codes not only provide models but also continually test us. Every time we respond "yes" or "no" to a fashion, an advertisement, a commodity, a poll, a television program, a news issue or a political candidate, our response is monitored.

Q **You mean like: "Are you watching day-time TV or not? Are you buying Pepsi or Coke? Are you for candidate X or Y? Are you wearing Calvin Klein or Jordache?"**

A Exactly. And such tests not only restrict our responses to "yes" or "no" but also determine our options, limiting the very scope of the issues and things we may choose from. Thus our lives are controlled by a system of binary regulation—where the question/answer option of the test has been reduced to an either/or binary code:

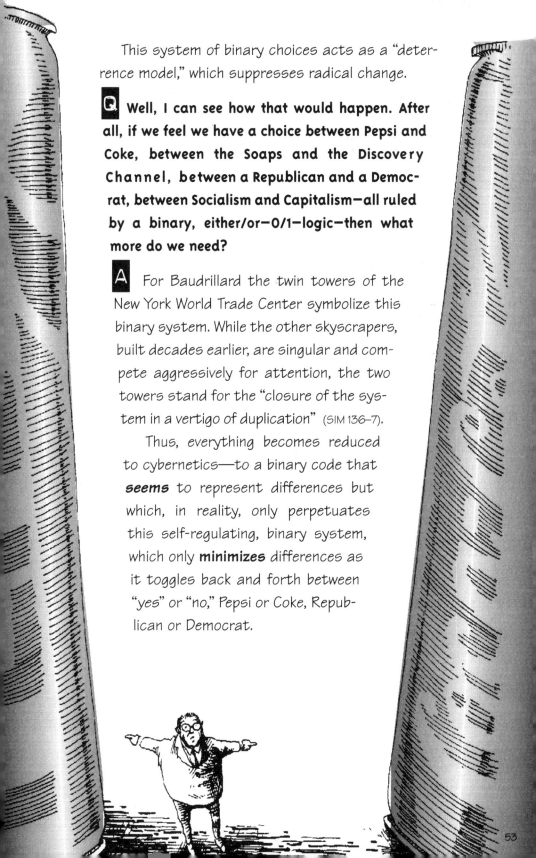

This system of binary choices acts as a "deterrence model," which suppresses radical change.

Q **Well, I can see how that would happen. After all, if we feel we have a choice between Pepsi and Coke, between the Soaps and the Discovery Channel, between a Republican and a Democrat, between Socialism and Capitalism—all ruled by a binary, either/or—0/1—logic—then what more do we need?**

A For Baudrillard the twin towers of the New York World Trade Center symbolize this binary system. While the other skyscrapers, built decades earlier, are singular and compete aggressively for attention, the two towers stand for the "closure of the system in a vertigo of duplication" (SIM 136–7).

Thus, everything becomes reduced to cybernetics—to a binary code that **seems** to represent differences but which, in reality, only perpetuates this self-regulating, binary system, which only **minimizes** differences as it toggles back and forth between "yes" or "no," Pepsi or Coke, Republican or Democrat.

Q To me it seems like the film *Jurassic Park*.

A How's that?

Q Because *Jurassic Park* is about people either passively accepting or refusing to buy into being passive observers of a spectacular, monstrous world of simulacra, of copies, generated ad infinitum by means of codes.

A That's brilliant! But you must also realize that your very example, the film *Jurassic Park*, is itself a monstrous simulacra generated ad infinitum via a code. But according to Baudrillard, people inculturated into Postmodern society are so surrounded by simulacra they no longer have a choice. Consider the case of Joe Player, an 18-year-old behind the wheel of a car. He is on a narrow mountain road. He is passing another car on a curve. He is doing 220, too fast to evade the oncoming truck that

seems to leap toward him. He slams on the brakes. He skids. Crash! The two vehicles go up in a burst of flame.

A second later the crash evaporates. Joe Player's

car reappears unscathed. He floors it, racing to pass another car just ahead of him. Joe Player is playing a video game. When he runs out of quarters he goes out into the parking lot, into his real car. But, as he pulls out into traffic, it doesn't seem real. Nor do the cars on the road. He feels that if he ran into them he would just eat them like Ms. Pacman eats dots. Joe Player is surfing the simulacrum.

Originally **simulacrum**, according to Plato, is the *false copy that overshadows our experience of the essential and Ideal Forms*. A cocker spaniel, a German shepherd, or a collie, for instance, would be, in Plato's philosophy, impure copies of a universal and Ideal Essence of Dogginess.

But in Baudrillard's view, Postmodernity has overthrown the very concept of true copy. And this has happened in stages.

Imagine the experience of a Christian nun in medieval Europe. She worships an icon of the Madonna. The icon reflects a divine feminine reality. The icon is a good, true copy because it is so close to the original that in her meditations the nun awakens to the spiritual presence behind the form. She could be called an idolater—a worshiper of an idol.

But the iconoclast sees things differently. She does not feel that images reveal divinity, but mask and pervert the divine. Therefore, such images are evil, bad copies, and should be destroyed.

A third perspective is that of the skeptic. He feels that the whole thing is a farce. The icon of the Madonna only hides the fact that there is no divine being—hides the absence of a divine being.

Finally, there is a fourth perspective. In the Postmodern era, icons, images, copies—simulations—bear no resemblance to any reality. In fact, **the simulation, the simulacrum, the copy, becomes the real!**

Q **You mean like there are a million copies not of the Madonna—but of Madonna—which become more real than Madonna the person?**

"Double click on my icon— and I'll show you what PO MO is all about!"

66 You see, it's like this. During the Middle Ages there were, like, a bunch of longbearded monks. They used to, like, hide away in their cells, like, y'know—and liked to like, dip their quills into, like, dark ink, and then copy down the words and phrases, and sentences and verses, of the Holy Word. These, like, words of

Holy Writ which they, like, wrote down, were only the outer expressions of a, like, deep **intercourse** they were having with the mystical Word that illumined their, like, prayers. But of course, all these, like, prayers were, like **dominated**, by a single image—that of the Holy, like, Virgin, the, like, Madonna.

Today, of course, it is not like, **the** Madonna who dominates, but, like, Madonna-like-**me**! Today it is like, **my** image that undulates forevermore, reproducing, like, infinitely, like, there are millions of me and like, and millions of my like belly buttons, like, bouncing back and forth before everyone's vision as if trying to like, decide between am I like a like Virgin or like a like Whore, in a like, erotic stream of images that MTV viewers, like, edit with like, Beavis and Butt-Head binary brains: they like think that my image, the image of my like, belly button, is either like, "cool" or like "sucks." It is the image of my belly button, not my belly button, which has become the real. **99**

THIS SUCKS.

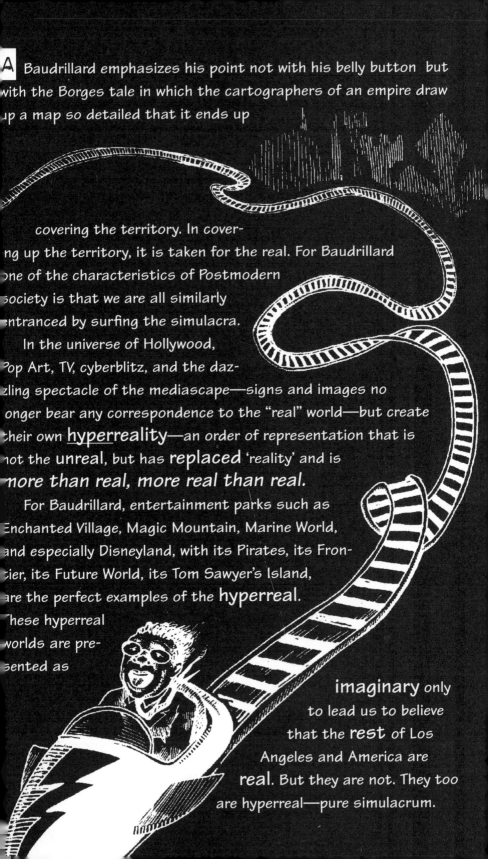

A Baudrillard emphasizes his point not with his belly button but with the Borges tale in which the cartographers of an empire draw up a map so detailed that it ends up

covering the territory. In covering up the territory, it is taken for the real. For Baudrillard one of the characteristics of Postmodern society is that we are all similarly entranced by surfing the simulacra.

In the universe of Hollywood, Pop Art, TV, cyberblitz, and the dazzling spectacle of the mediascape—signs and images no longer bear any correspondence to the "real" world—but create their own <u>hyperreality</u>—an order of representation that is not the **unreal**, but has **replaced** 'reality' and is *more than real, more real than real.*

For Baudrillard, entertainment parks such as Enchanted Village, Magic Mountain, Marine World, and especially Disneyland, with its Pirates, its Frontier, its Future World, its Tom Sawyer's Island, are the perfect examples of the **hyperreal**. These hyperreal worlds are presented as **imaginary** only to lead us to believe that the **rest** of Los Angeles and America are **real**. But they are not. They too are hyperreal—pure simulacrum.

What Baudrillard calls the Death of the Real arouses nostalgic attempts to resurrect the real. Baudrillard sees Watergate as one such attempt. For parading the scandalous illegalities of the Nixon administration implies, falsely, that these affronts to democracy represent a deviation from the norm—and that the system of government in general respects law and morality.

The Death of the Real also inspires a proliferation of **myths of origin**. Thus, in 1971, the government of the Philippines re-situated a small tribe of Tasaday Indians to their original jungle home. Here, according to the government's ethnologists, the tribe could live uncorrupted by civilization. Baudrillard argues, however, that in removing the Tasaday from modern civilization, ethnology simultaneously ignores the **real** Tasaday—who want to remain living among TV's and cars—and create a mere **model**, a simulacrum of what an "original" pre-civilized tribe **"should"** look like—**before ethnology**!

I AM NOT A . . .

Q In other words, this representation of what a tribe should look like was created only by ethnology?

A Yes. And this attempt to resurrect the real, the original, has also taken place at the caves of Lascaux in southern France. It was here, during the closing millennia of the last Glacial Age, that teeming herds of magnificent grazing animals passed in waves across the vast post-glacial landscape, occasionally falling prey to the hunting tribes that depended upon the herds for their subsistence. And it was here, in the subterranean caves, that primitive artists painted magnificent forms, bison, mammoths, rhinoceroses.

Yet today 500 meters from the original caves—an exact replica of the caves has been created in order to preserve the original. It has become more real than the real cave. And in the same way, modern science recently has geared up to save the mummy of Ramses II.

Thus, with the Death of the Real, the **hyperreal** takes over—Disneyland, The Tasaday, Watergate, the Lascaux simulacrum—more real than the real itself.

And with **hyperreality** all the potentially political, explosive, polar antagonisms that had inhabited and animated the Real collapse into one another—**implode**—especially in the political realm!

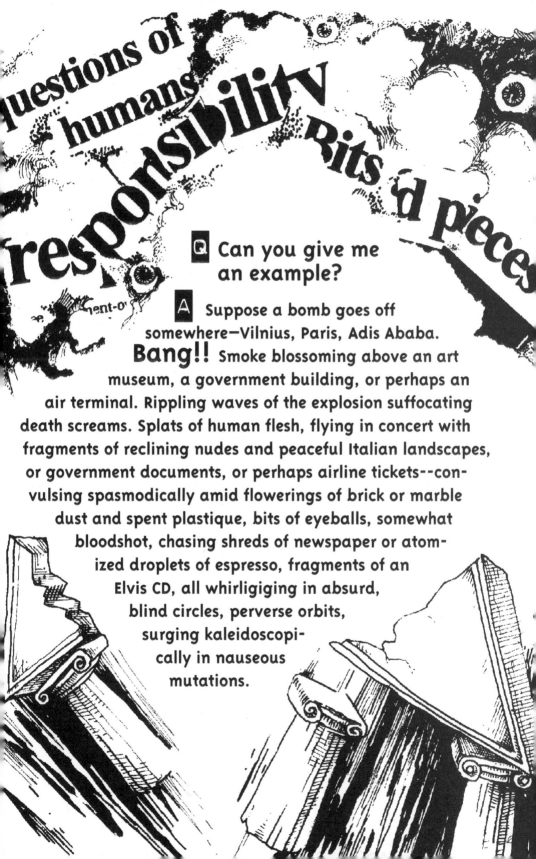

Q Can you give me an example?

A Suppose a bomb goes off somewhere—Vilnius, Paris, Adis Ababa. **Bang!!** Smoke blossoming above an art museum, a government building, or perhaps an air terminal. Rippling waves of the explosion suffocating death screams. Splats of human flesh, flying in concert with fragments of reclining nudes and peaceful Italian landscapes, or government documents, or perhaps airline tickets--convulsing spasmodically amid flowerings of brick or marble dust and spent plastique, bits of eyeballs, somewhat bloodshot, chasing shreds of newspaper or atomized droplets of espresso, fragments of an Elvis CD, all whirligiging in absurd, blind circles, perverse orbits, surging kaleidoscopically in nauseous mutations.

Q Who did it?

A That's just the question Baudrillard asks. Leftist extremists?
Right-wing skinheads? Centrists seeking to discredit the extremes?
Corrupt police appealing to the public need for security? **The
answer(s),** says Baudrillard, **have nothing to do with the facts.** All
the media responses and interpretations are already preprogrammed
and all orbit, whirligiging, in absurd, perverse, nauseous circles, orbiting
around the merest fact—according to established codes or models.

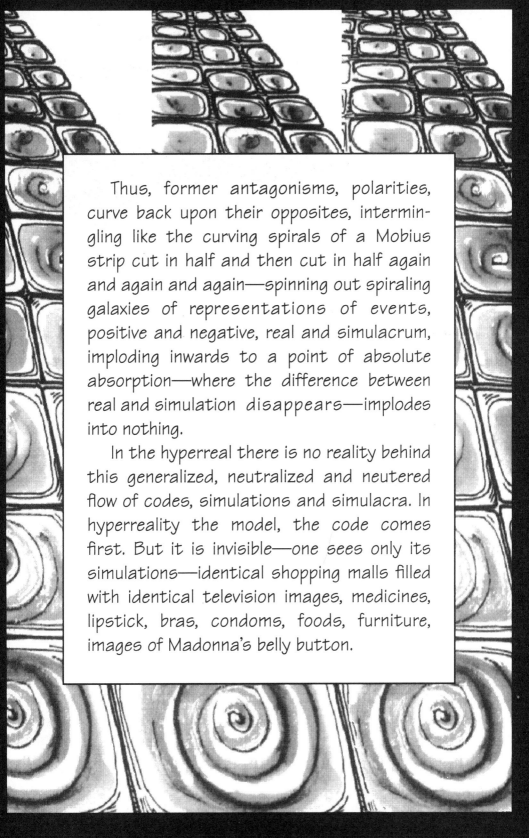

Thus, former antagonisms, polarities, curve back upon their opposites, intermingling like the curving spirals of a Mobius strip cut in half and then cut in half again and again and again—spinning out spiraling galaxies of representations of events, positive and negative, real and simulacrum, imploding inwards to a point of absolute absorption—where the difference between real and simulation disappears—implodes into nothing.

In the hyperreal there is no reality behind this generalized, neutralized and neutered flow of codes, simulations and simulacra. In hyperreality the model, the code comes first. But it is invisible—one sees only its simulations—identical shopping malls filled with identical television images, medicines, lipstick, bras, condoms, foods, furniture, images of Madonna's belly button.

Like the Beavis and Butt-Head episode in which the two, watching TV, watch the cops break in the door and bust them—live!—but they are too glued to the tube to realize that it is they, themselves, that are being busted—that the whole thing is taking place live—that the cops and the camera have busted into their living room. Life has become TV, and TV, life. TV watches us, and we watch TV watching over us. It watches over us like whirligigs of DNA, orbiting around us, governing the mutations of the real into the hyperreal. TV and life, real and hyperreal, contract, collapse, telescope, implode into simulation.

In hyperreality antagonisms and polar dichotomies dissolve. A generalized deterrence is generated. Atomic war will never happen. The hyperreal media spectacle of the nuclear arms race and the space race imploded the antagonisms of the superpowers toward a peaceful co-existence.

And in orbit, floating freely above all antagonisms, the ultimate end product of the space race is the cool, lunar, hyper-simulation: the Lunar module.

In The Shadow of The Silent Majorities

Q But what other effects has this had on society?

A In another book, *In the Shadow of the Silent Majorities* (SSM 1978), Baudrillard contends that what had been society has imploded into a hyperconformist body obsessed so much with spectacle that it would rather watch TV than take political action. It becomes electrified only by computer networks and electronic media—by which it is so polled, tested, and hyped by models that it has become inert and bored. But at the same time it is hyper, passive, resistant, demanding even more moonshots, rock spectaculars, mass entertainments—yet suspicious and sceptical, apathetic because it realizes that any attempt to change the system will simply be co-opted by the system for its own ends.

All this has signaled the death of the social.

On Seduction

In his next book, **On Seduction**, Baudrillard talks about love. Courtly love, in the medieval courts of southern France in the 11th century, was an involved and elaborate ritual requiring the exchange of love poems, blushes behind floral fans, eyes suddenly downcast after casting a sly sidelong glance, kisses blown from the ramparts of castles, implications, half unveilings, double entendres, titillations, whispers, jealousies, adroit evasions, feigned refusals, feints, fainting, half-surrenderings ..

Such moves in the game of courtly love were aristocratic, artificial and symbolic—delighting in the play of the game itself. The game relied upon infinite deferral—in the putting off of actual sex—in prolonging the art and artifice of seduction. And for Baudrillard, seduction is feminine.

Sex, on the other hand, Baudrillard regards as a masculine mode—always centered on the phallus, natural, non-artificial.

Freud was right: there is only one single sexuality, one single libido—masculine. Sexuality is this distinct structure which is discriminating, centered on the phallus, castration, the name of the father, repression.

There isn't any other. It serves no purpose to dream of some non-phallic sexuality that is neither barred nor marked (SED 16).

Since seduction is composed of the artifice of signs and gestures, it is a form of mastery over the symbolic universe.

Sexuality, on the other hand, is not cultural but natural—a form of mastery over the real universe. Feminine seduction relies on artifice—makeup, fashion, the display of a shoulder or breast beneath black lace. And it is only through such seduction that the masculine can be subverted!

This is hot seduction. But there is also, for Baudrillard, a cool seduction—the seduction of simulacra—of films, radio, the idols of the silver or Technicolor screen—a self-seduction in which we seduce ourselves by immersing ourselves in a play of signs, simulations, images that escape male sexuality.

In his next book Baudrillard continues his meditations on Postmodern culture, by taking a road trip to the most Postmodern of Postmodern cultures—America.

America

In the early 19th century the French count Alexis de Tocqueville took a trip to the New World, which provided material for one of his best-known works: *Democracy in America*. He wrote that he found America rich in

democracy, but poor in civilization.

In the 1970s and 1980s Baudrillard followed in de Tocqueville's footsteps, providing, in *America*, a Postmodern simulation of de Tocqueville's

account. Baudrillard's travelogue also conforms to the more recent French fixations on such Americana as the desert, the American Wild West, Le Jazz—mystifying various aspects of America as essentially primitive and savage.

Baudrillard's road trip, speeding past endless vistas of road signs, neon lights, empty desert landscapes, motels, reveals an America of surface glitter, vanishing into emptiness. In fact, the title of an important chapter is "Vanishing Point," referring to **the Death of Meaning, the Death of Reality, the Death of the Social, the Death of the Political, and the Death of Sexuality** in

the Postmodern uni-
verse— these "realities" re-
cede into a vanishing point in
Baudrillard's rearview mirror on
his drive through Death Valley, In
fact, Baudrillard's travelogue
begins with the warning one finds
on some rearview mirrors: Cau-
tion: Objects in this mirror may
be closer than they appear! (A 9)

The realities of the pre-simu-
lacrum era vanishing like mirages
in a rearview mirror is an apoca-
lyptic vision—a vision of the end
of the world. For Baudrillard this
vision of America is the model
for the rest of the world—
the code for an emerging
hyperreal and simu-
lated supra-
modern

world. Because of this America is
"the center of the world." And
America is a desert—especially in
its cities—a place where "real life"
has vanished into a kind of glittering, empty non-culture. And
this empty, dry, sterile, lunar
desert of astral America, the
desert of meaningful society,
empty as a TV tuned to a dead
channel—whether in its landscapes or cityscapes, whether in
the insane movement of joggers,
traffic and pedestrians in Los
Angeles, bodies circulating on
freeways or plugged into computer circuits, whether in the utopia
of California, of Santa Barbara or
of Santa Cruz, the paradise of
California with its intellectuals,
freeways and film stars, whether
in the great neon whore of Las
Vegas, the "wall-to-wall prostitu-
tion" of New York, with its
plumes of smoke like
"girls wringing out
their hair

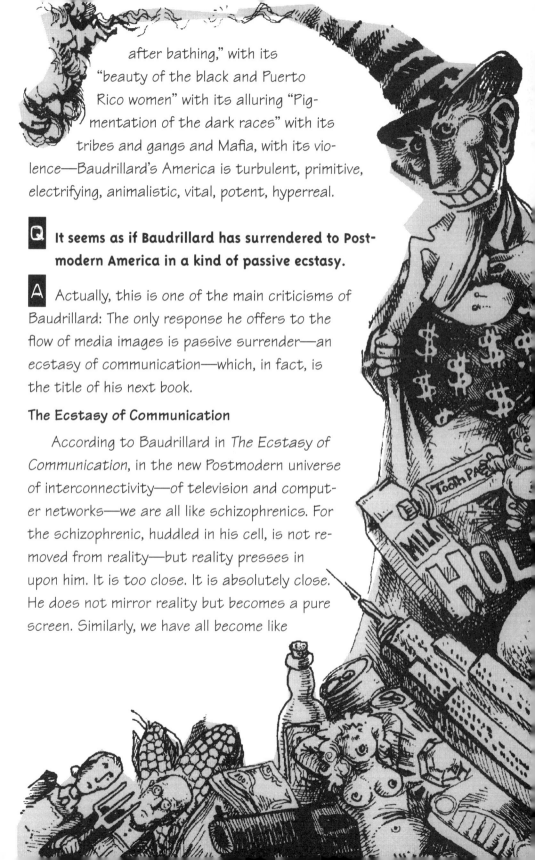

after bathing," with its "beauty of the black and Puerto Rico women" with its alluring "Pigmentation of the dark races" with its tribes and gangs and Mafia, with its violence—Baudrillard's America is turbulent, primitive, electrifying, animalistic, vital, potent, hyperreal.

Q **It seems as if Baudrillard has surrendered to Postmodern America in a kind of passive ecstasy.**

A Actually, this is one of the main criticisms of Baudrillard: The only response he offers to the flow of media images is passive surrender—an ecstasy of communication—which, in fact, is the title of his next book.

The Ecstasy of Communication

According to Baudrillard in *The Ecstasy of Communication*, in the new Postmodern universe of interconnectivity—of television and computer networks—we are all like schizophrenics. For the schizophrenic, huddled in his cell, is not removed from reality—but reality presses in upon him. It is too close. It is absolutely close. He does not mirror reality but becomes a pure screen. Similarly, we have all become like television and computer screens— those luminous eyes illuminating and penetrating even our most private spaces with an obscene pressure. And this promiscuous invasion of our former privacy is both ecstatic and obscene. The obscenity not of the hidden but of the all-too-visual. The obscenity that no longer harbors any secret. An obscene ecstasy—a cool-lunar seductive, electric pornography of excessive images and information feeding upon us, penetrating all our private spaces, the obscenity of fascination, like a pornographic close-up, producing a state of giddiness to which we surrender in an Ecstasy of Communication.

But Baudrillard informs us in his introduction that *Ecstasy* is only a simulation model of some of his earlier books—a simulation in which Baudrillard out-Baudrillards himself—becoming more Baudrillard than Baudrillard. We must not forget that in the French cultural scene theories are just like commodities—they are in competition with other theories in the French cultural marketplace. And Baudrillard understands that the best way to make his theories competitive is to transform them into hyperreal simulations of theory. To spin out Jurassic

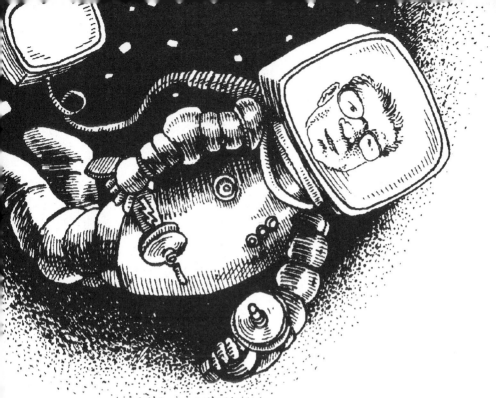

Park monsters of theory. Baudrillard's understanding of the media has made him an effective competitor—a kind of celebrity—because his attacks on his fellow French intellectuals are hyperreal spectacles meant for public consumption, tending more and more toward a kind of vanishing point. For instance, he has been criticized, but also made famous, by hyperreal statements such as "The Gulf War never happened." In fact, some critics claim that Baudrillard, in his later work, is actually doing science fiction instead of Postmodern theory.

Q **But it seems that Postmodern theory would have to be similar to science fiction, since the impact of technologies on cultures is so intense.**

A That's true. In fact, some Postmodern thinkers say that certain science fiction writers do a better job at describing the impact of cybertechnologies than does Baudrillard. But that is a topic we can return to later.

Modernist Architecture

Q **Well, it's all rather dizzying—all these hyperrealities and whirligiging simulacra. It reminds me of Jameson becoming so disoriented in the Bonaventure Hotel. What is it about Postmodern architecture that is so dizzying?**

A It's a good question, because architecture is actually the realm in which Postmodernism began. But in order to understand what Postmodern architecture is, we have to know something about modern architecture. Modernism in architecture began with the Bauhaus school, founded in Weimar, Germany, in 1919 by Walter Gropius. Here artists such as Paul Klee and Vassily Kandinsky combined their architectural studies with courses in painting, crafts, drama and typography. The school believed that buildings should be functional. They also developed what came to be known as the International Style, an attempt to unite architecture, the fine arts and mass-production technology.

The manifesto of architectural modernism, *Towards a New Architecture*, was published in Paris in 1923, and translated into English

A HOUSE IS A HOUSE IS A HOUSE.

BUT IS IT A HOME?

in 1927. The author, a kind of messiah of Modernist architecture, was Le Corbusier, actually the pen name of one Charles-Edouard Jeanneret (1887–1965). He was a well-traveled native of Switzerland, who was to establish himself as a city planner, architect, designer, painter, sculptor and prophet of a new architectural creed.

Le Corbusier gained his pen name by virtue of the fact that his face resembled that of a raven (*corbeau*). And, just like Poe's raven, who, in Poe's words, said "Nevermore," Le Corbusier also said, "Nevermore!"

No more retro, ancient, cluttered, nineteenth-century styles. No more custom. No more inherited designs. No more gloomy interiors jammed with bunches of useless bric-a-brac, no more heavy furniture, chandeliers, mantel-pieces, thick carpets. No more elaborate bookcases, consoles, china cabinets, dressers, sideboards, draped curtains, cushions, canopies, damasked wallpapers, carved furniture, faded and arty colors, mirrored wardrobes. No more decoration, ornament, symbolism. No more heterogeneity, ambiguity, capriciousness, riot, stitching together of unrelated elements. No more garlands, exquisite ovals, triangular doves preening themselves, boudoirs embellished with poofs of gold and black velvet, no more stifling elegancies! quoth Le Corbusier—

Nevermore!

Just as the prophet of literary modernism, Ezra Pound, had proclaimed "Make it new," Le Corbusier believed that architecture should use new materials such as steel and reinforced concrete, and new construction techniques. This new architecture was to be rational. It should exhibit a grandeur of a mathematical order, for by turning to mathematical calculations, it would reveal universal law—the principles that govern our universe. The new architectural designs should be intelligent, cold and calm—pure creations of the mind—manifestations of men creating their own universe.

If buildings can be read like books, Le Corbusier called for a Platonic vocabulary of pure, absolute forms: cubes, cones, spheres, cylinders, pyramids, squares. All this based on a Platonic attitude that knowledge properly resides in pure, eternal, absolute "Ideal Forms," which we can know with our intellects, though not through our senses.

For instance, it will always be true and knowable that 2 + 2 = 4. And this will always be true even if there are no longer 2 + 2 apples or oranges to add up to four.

Believing that architectural beauty should be based on the same immutable, eternal Platonic primary forms, he liked structures such as the Pyramids, the Temple of Luxor, the towers of Babylon, the Coliseum, Hadrian's

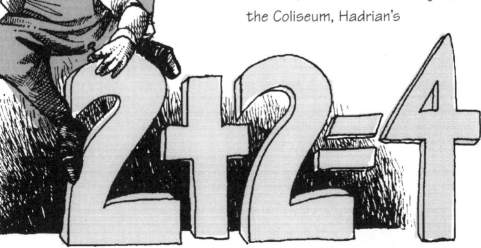

villa, Constantinople's Santa Sophia, the Mosques of Stamboul, the Tower of Pisa, the copulas of Michelangelo. But above all else—the Parthenon. The Parthenon is perfect. Le Corbusier found in it brutality, intensity, sweetness, delicacy and strength. It is the climax of "pure forms in precise relationship"—bestowing upon truth and emotion "superior and mathematical order." Modern architecture thus attempted to pare down line, space and form to their pure essentials.

If Le Corbusier has a hero it is the engineer— the creator of bridges, of Atlantic liners, of railways. Engineers, like Cubist painters, are not distracted with ornamentation but satisfy our spirits by reducing their creations to pure geometric, mathematical, Platonic forms. Engineers are virile, useful. Their minds, absorbed in mathematical calculations and the perception of primary geometric forms, are in harmony with natural law.

If architects could be more like engineers, then buildings would rise up like pure creations of spirit—ringing in unison with universal order. Down with frivolous ornamentation! If you must have diversity—then let it emerge from the interplay of primary forms! Let architecture be the correct and magnificent play of such masses brought together in light! Let light shine on the great primary forms of p r i s m s, cubes, cones, spheres, cylinders, pyramids. Let homes be machines for living with terraces instead of roofs, with windows all around, without clutter—but with built-in furnishings, without gaudy chandeliers, but with diffused electric lighting, and built of standardized materials like cars, cannons, airplanes! Let great new utopian vertical cities, cities of towers, whose immense geometrical glass facades reflect the sky, rise in skyscrapers amid green plantations of trees. Let these skyscrapers contain the brains of the nation. Clear away Paris's narrow streets to admit wide, noble spaces, populated with trees. Let the suburbs be garden cities where people can play ball, and garden. Let all the cities of Europe be torn down and reconstructed in the image of American cities.

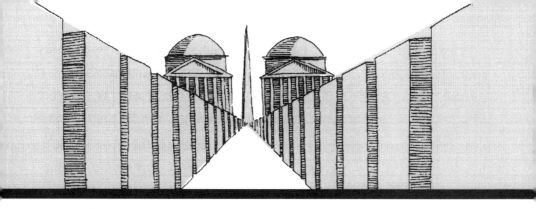

Postmodern Architcture and Art

By 1950, many of the elements of this International Style had, indeed, become international—the simplified, concentrated lines and forms, the emphasis on function as beauty, the essential mathematical harmony of pure forms, the celebration of rational, progressive tendencies, the adoption of new technologies and new materials, the yearning for a spiritual holism of space and form, the distaste for bazaar-like, arbitrary reproduction of historic styles.

Yet—what it all boiled down to was cityscapes full of concrete and glass boxes. And what was modern architecture to do—based as it was on eternal mathematical harmony—if the supposed perfection of mathematics itself broke down into non-Euclidean geometries and incompleteness theorems? And what was modern architecture to do if its huge, utopian projects—such as Brazilia—flopped? What if the world was growing tired of failed utopias? Then the utopian theories and the architectural projects that reflected them would have to change—and that change would need a new voice. And that new voice was **Charles Jencks.**

Charles Jencks

Charles Jencks is an architectural critic who has been engaged in the often heated debate between modernist and Postmodernist architects about whether Postmodern architecture should even exist. He is also a major voice in the ongoing attempt to define Postmodernism. In fact, his book, *The Language of Postmodern Architecture* (1977), was the first work to attempt to thematize the Postmodern and to use "Postmodern" in the title.

In his subsequent books *What is Postmodernism?* and *Postmodernism*, he traces the history of the concept. Originally used by the Spanish writer Federico De Onis in 1934 to describe a poetic reaction to modernist poetry, the term was subsequently used, in 1975, by the historian Arnold Toynbee to designate pluralism and the rise of non-Western cultures.

In the 1960s the early roots of Postmodernism got started by a group of English intellectuals, the Independent Group, who were fascinated with American culture: TV, movies, ads, machinery and commercial culture. They created pop collages of such objects—the first pop art. In America, in the midst of Hippies and Yuppies, Andy Warhol cranked out a bunch of images of mass culture: Marilyn Monroe, Jackie Kennedy, a Campbell's Soup can. Then, in the 1970s the Postmodern movement became more academic and respectable: in 1971 Ihab Hassan published an essay, "POSTmodernISM A Paracritical Bibliography," and the Postmodernist movement was officially inaugurated in theory—celebrating writers such as William Burroughs, Jean Genet, James Joyce and Samuel Beckett, the music of John Cage and the futurists Marshall McLuhan and Buckminster Fuller.

But according to Jencks, these artists and architects were really Late modernists, not Postmodernists.

Q Late Modernists?

A Yes. Because authors such as James Joyce were writing things, such as Finnegan's Wake, that very few people could understand. And that's what a lot of Late modernists—or High modernists did. Composers like John Cage were writing "music" that nobody understood based on what most people would call noise, or pure silence. In one piece he remains poised over the piano for several minutes, as if to strike the opening chord of a concert—and

the composition consists of the sound of the audience waiting for the concert to begin. And thinkers such as Bucky Fuller were designing according to the utopian assumptions of modernism.

AS ON YOUR FACE PLAIN THE NOSE THAT RUNS AND DRIPS MAKES ITS WHEEZING SELF, MY WORK.

More to Jencks's liking is novelist Umberto Eco's recognition of a double element in Postmodernism. For Jencks and Eco Postmodernism is modernism

HEY, IT'S THE DUKE WHO LOVES YOU MADLY.

along with a Postmodern relationship to the past: "The postmodern reply to the modern consists of recognizing that the past, since it cannot really be destroyed, because its destruction leads to silence, must be revisited: but with irony, not innocently. I think of the postmodern attitude as that of a man who loves a very cultivated woman and knows he cannot say to her, I love you madly, because he knows that she knows (and that she knows that he knows) that these words have already been written by Barbara Cartland. Still, there is a solution. He can say, "As Barbara Cartland would put it, I love you madly." At this point, having avoided false innocence, having said clearly that it is no longer possible to speak innocently, he will nevertheless have said what he wanted to say to the woman: that he loves her, but he loves her in an age of lost innocence. If the woman goes along with this, she will have received a declaration of love all the same. Neither of the two speakers will feel innocent, both will have accepted the challenge of the past, of the already said, which cannot be eliminated; both will consciously and with pleasure play the game of irony. ... But both will have succeeded, once again, in speaking of love." (ELO, PNR 67–8)

And this fits in with Jencks's definition of Postmodernism as *"double coding: the combination of Modern techniques with something else (usually traditional building) in order for architecture to communicate with the public and a concerned minority, usually other architects"* (WIP 14).

A typical Postmodern building creates a **double coding** through **eclecticism**: by putting together two different styles of two different periods, it creates parody, ambiguity, contradiction, paradox. For, in Jencks's view, a building is not just a building but something like a language. A building can be read like a book. It has connotations and allusions. It signifies. It has meanings—and often says two or more things at the same time.

Thus Postmodern architects must be **both** popular **and** professionally based. For instance, the colorful handrails in the Stuttgart museum appeal to the popular tastes of kids dressed in Day-Glo colors, while its classicism— its quotations of pure Greek forms—appeals to the highbrow elitist.

Postmodern architecture must use both new techniques and old patterns. Postmodernist architects are, then, not simply revivalists who simply bring back the past and stop using modernism. They use modernism and yet go beyond it. They quote from the past, but with irony. They parody the past. They use pastiche. Thus double coding, like Eco's "I love you madly," stages the dissonance and play between past and present. This dissonance can be ironic, humorous, parodic, playful, allusive—but it makes the "reader" of the building reflect. The "reader" becomes something of an architectural critic.

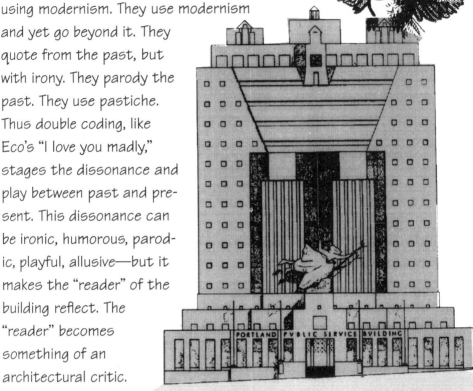

TWEET

PORTLAND PVBLIC SERVICE BVILDING

Because of this, doing Postmodern architecture is one way to do Postmodern theory—its double coding makes it interesting not only to the average Joe Blow on the street but also to fellow architects and Postmodern critics.

Even an object as simple as a teapot can be double coded. Designer Michael Graves designed a teapot that has simple, functional modernist lines but flaunts an ornamental bird for the whistle—a kind of aural pun.

In 1980 Michael Graves—the same guy who designed the teapot with the whistling bird—won a competition for his design for the Portland Public Services Building. It is radically eclectic and double coded—its glass hints that it is a public space; its size and ornamental garlands suggest Egyptian and baroque motifs; its use of a sculpture,

"Portlandia", over the front door—creates a playful mood. But the building was attacked by modernists who criticized it for what they called its lack of discipline—its jukebox-over-sized-Christmas-package look. Supporters, on the other hand, commented that it related to the nearby City Hall as well as other pre-modernist and modernist buildings in the neighborhood.

Q **But why should we even have Postmodern architecture?**

A Because huge utopian modernist housing projects alienated the very inhabitants they were designed to house. These planned utopias turned into wastelands of graffiti, vandalism and neglect. Thus in the late 1960s and early 1970s they were dynamited. In fact Jencks, in a public lecture, proclaimed that on **July 15, 1972, at 3:32 PM, modern architecture died**, as a huge housing project in St. Louis was blown to smithereens.

Modernists were alarmed, of course, and immediately began denouncing the new Postmodernism with religious fervor. But, according to Jencks, the modernist attacks on Postmodern architecture actually invigorated its growth. For instance, when it was announced in a column in *Le Monde* in October of 1981 that "a spectre is haunting Europe, the spectre of Postmodernism," most Frenchmen just shrugged, bit into their croissants and flipped the page. But modernists didn't simply shrug off the announcement; their panic effectively inflated the spectre into a full-fledged movement. Therefore, reasons Jencks, there must have existed a hidden resent-ment to modernism all along.

The death of architectural modernism may have saved a lot of inner cities, where the modernist tendency would have been to bulldoze them and construct more utopian housing units. What Postmodernism offered was eclectic, incremental regeneration—that is to say, *regenerating*, slowly using the mix of what is already there along with what is new.

For Jencks modernism had been something of a religious phenomenon. After all, it declared ornamentation heretical, and viewed itself as the universal International Style using new construction techniques and new materials. It had a mission to transform society.

According to Jencks, modernist buildings, such as the Chicago Civic Center or Chicago's Lake Shore housing units,

1972—is a book called **Learning from Las Vegas.** This book criticizes the utopian, progressive elements of architectural modernism. It criticizes modernism's attempt to build glass and steel boxes, to define architecture as enclosed space. If space is sacred to modernism, then painting, sculpture and literature, mere decoration, are opposed to pure space. Modernist architects rejected an entire tradition of architecture in which paintings, sculpture and graphics were integrated with architecture. Modernist buildings had attempted to symbolize nothing but ideal geometric forms. In idealizing the well-engineered geometric forms of Transatlantic steamships, American grain elevators, and Cubist paintings, they had ended up symbolizing a brave new world of science and technology—a nautical-industrial-Cubist world.

attempt to be nothing more than simple geometric forms—glass and steel and concrete boxes—which in their squareness say "this is what I am—a square box—and nothing else." The form does not refer to or allude to or mean anything outside itself.

Postmodernist architecture, on the other hand, rejects such simplicity. Postmodern buildings reflect and refer to their environment. If Le Corbusier was the Messiah of modernist architecture, Robert Venturi, Denise Scott Brown and Steven Izenour are the prophets of Postmodern architecture. And their manifesto, first published in

D o w n   with the   universal! proclaim Venturi, Scott Brown and Izenour.

Accept the clutter of mixed, mass-culture, ornamented, ticky-tacky, suburban, Gingerbread, New Orleans, French Provincial and Ranch styles. Down with the architecture of space, form and function. Bring in the icons of Pop Art, of advertising, of everyday commercial o b j e c t s - - o f Campbell's soup cans in a gallery, or of images from comic strip art, to suggest satire, sorrow and irony.

Let the architect become a jester! Let architecture, like the pop art of Warhol and Leichtenstein, use familiar motifs--designing non-authoritarian buildings that instead of saying "I am a square" say many things at once. Let Postmodern buildings express irony, along with comedy, sorrow, paradox, and the un-

authoritarian qualities needed for living humorously in a society made up of different races, sexual orientations, classes and cultures.

For we do live in a pluralist society, reflected in mixed, glittering, flashing bazaars of neon lights and signs on the Las Vegas Strip, the hodgepodge of contradictory, competing and conflicting styles, the roadsigns and billboards that whiz by in a blur of complex meanings, a roadscape/carscape in which the mix of symbols is more important than pure form --the dazzling pictorial themes of the casinos (the flamboyant

Flamingo, the Desert Inn, the exotic Tropicana, the arabesque Aladdin, Caesar's Palace, the Stardust, like the facades of Gothic cathedrals, almost all sign and symbol) the casino shopping malls like oriental bazaars. Las Vegas Strip architecture is a grab-bag, eclectic, a l l u s i v e , paradoxical--the Aladdin is Tudor with a Moorish facade. Caesar's Palace is Early Christian, Roman, Neo-Classical, Motel Moderne, Etruscan and Miesian. Motifs, signs, columns, wings, formations and floors parody and question each other.

The Las Vegas Strip is an inclusive order. There is no one dominant theme. No expert. But the spectator strolls

past a heterogeneous playground of multiple, vital, incongruous, chaotic, intertextual, allusive urban signs, meanings, orders-- all exploring the architecture of the past.

Let architecture be fun! Turn staid architectural notions topsy-turvy! Indulgently embrace complexity, mixing images and symbols from the historical past in a nostalgic collage! Let image determine form! Let development be based on incremental, diverse growth, rather than utopian plans! Let buildings reflect the diversity of users and clients' tastes! Let architects design for specific persons--rather than from some utopian, abstract conception of Man. Let Postmodern buildings fit in with the buildings surrounding them!

According to the authors of *Learning from Los Vegas*:

"The emerging order of the Strip is a complex order. It is not the easy, rigid order of the urban renewal project or the fashionable 'total design' of the megastructure...It is not an order dominated by the expert and made easy for the eye. The moving eye in the moving body must work to pick out and interpret a variety of changing, juxtaposed orders" (LLV 135-6).

In Jencks's view, Postmodern architecture displays 10 characteristics. Let us use Philip Johnson's AT&T building in New York City as an example.

It is pluralistic—radically eclectic—celebrating difference and otherness. It quotes different styles and languages. The AT&T building transforms the traditional glass and steel skyscraper into a grandfather clock topped off with a Chippendale broken pediment.

This eclecticism leads to a dissonant beauty, a disharmonious harmony, an oxymoron, a paradox. After all, there is dissonance between a building and a clock. But his dissonance is humorous because many buildings display clocks.

The AT&T building displays an urbane urbanism. It doesn't stand out alone. It looks pretty much like other modernist skyscrapers, but it blends into, mirrors, mocks, parodies and extends other buildings in the environment.

Postmodern buildings are anthropomorphic—their ornaments and moldings often suggest the human form. The AT&T building does not do this, but suggests indirectly, through mimicking a human artifact—a clock.

It displays a relationship between past and present—grandfather clock and modern sky-scraper. This putting to-gether of styles can bring the past face to face with the present, which allows the architect not only to recol-lect past styles but also to paro-dy them, to in-voke nostalgia and indulge in pastiche.

There is a yearning for con-tent, for meaning. Instead of just saying "glass and steel box" the building also says "grandfa-ther clock."

There is double coding through the juxtaposition of styles—grandfather clock and modernist skyscraper—so that irony, ambiguity, and con-tradiction emerge. Post-modern buildings say not "either/or" but "both/and." The AT&T building says "both/and" by combining the contemporary (skyscraper) with the antique (grandfather clock), the functional (office build-ing) and the decorative (Chippendale broken pedi-ment) in an ironic double coding. It can mean two things at once.

Postmodern buildings are multivalent—they can mean many things simultaneously. Unlike the univalence of modernist buildings, which only say one thing—"I am a square"—Postmodern architecture is multivalent, non-exclusive, allusive, resonant, symbolic.

Postmodern architecture reinterprets tradition. It does not merely copy the past but reinterprets it. The AT&T building does not simply revive the past; it mocks it playfully.

Many Postmodern buildings yearn to return to the absent center—to a central communal space. But then realize that there is nothing we have in common to fill it with. So why not fill it with a clock?

Jencks defines Postmodern classicism as a revival drawing upon motifs from Greece and Rome. He identifies five streams of Postmodern classicism:

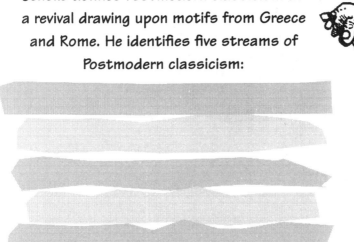

Metaphysical Classicism

Melancholic classicism is a mode of metaphysical classicism that focuses on a return to the urban, as symbolized by the Italian city square—the piazza—but with a difference. Postmodern architects such as Leon Krier and Postmodern artists such as Rito Wolff render such piazzas melancholy— because the piazzas are deserted. Yet, there is a yearning for a center here—and there is a center—but the center is empty.

Narrative Classicism

Traditional narrative painting depicts the heroic actions of great men—such as Socrates drinking the hemlock. They are meant to inspire. The Postmodern narrative painting often paints unheroic men engaged in immoral actions.

In Paul George's My Kent State, a vulnerable, nude muse—symbol of freedom— attempts to flee the scene of students being slayed.

This genre can take on erotic and subversive overtones, as in Eric Fischl's Bad Boy, a lad watching a nude woman while he steals from her purse.

Allegorical Classicism

Grant Drumheller's *Lightning Thrower* repeats the pose of a famous statue of Poseidon against a dreadful background of what Jencks calls "radioactive gloom." Do the flashings in the background signify a nuclear war brought on by Poseidon, Thor and Jupiter nuclear missiles?

A sub-genre—naive realism—returns to the innocence of Grant Wood and Grandma Moses. An example is David Ligare's *Woman in a Greek Chair*.

Realist Classicism

Realist classicism is always something of a paradox, an oxymoron or contradiction. In the classicist tradition the individual particulars of a body—the hands, torso, head, etc.—rendered in stone, were subordinated to Ideal beauty.

In realist classicism the scale is tipped toward the ugly, realistic aspects of the subject, which the pure classicist overlooks. Example? Works such as Philip Pearlstein's *Two Female Models on Brentwood Loveseat and Rug*. According to Jencks, "A parody of

sexuality is suggested by the way vast stretches of the body are focused on, as in a *Playboy* centerfold, only to be turned into sacks of sagging meat" (PM 127).

The Classical Sensibility

Jencks finds that some artists are faithful to a general spirit of classicism—they exhibit a classical sensibility in their works—even though their subjects are contemporary. Milet Andrejevic's *Apollo and Daphne*, for example, retells the Greek myth of Apollo chasing Daphne to the river, only to see her father, the River God, transform her into a laurel tree. It is double coded in that there is an ironic putting together of Vassar-type coeds, a post-hippie guitarist and a classical theme.

Poststructuralism

Q **Who are some other Postmodern theorists?**

A Well, some of the most important ones are Poststructuralist thinkers.

Q **Poststructuralist?**

A Poststructuralism is a movement associated with a wave of French thinkers: Jacques Derrida, Julia Kristeva, Roland Barthes, Gilles Deleuze, Felix Guattari and Michel Foucault. Poststructuralists tend to regard all knowledge—history, anthropology, literature, psychology, etc.—as textual. This means that knowledge is composed not just of **concepts** but also of **words**. Poststructuralists focus on reading the **written** condition of the text. Read in this manner, texts produce a variety of mutually contradictory effects.

Postmodernists also tend to think that language and meaning are fragmentary. We know that Postmodernism questions the whole notion of dominance. For instance, it questions the idea that one grand story can dominate smaller ones. It questions the idea that there is a hierarchy of stories, with the grand narratives on top and the smaller ones lower down on the totem pole. Poststructuralism backs up Postmodernism with its analysis of language and knowledge. One of the most prominent Poststructuralists has been a French intellectual named Michel Foucault.

Michel Foucault (and Baudrillard on Foucault)

Q Foucault?

A Michel Foucault was a French psychologist born in Poitiers in 1926. He was concerned with the relationship between **power** and **knowledge**. But he ridiculed the idea that power is a huge, monolithic state structure and was distrustful of big metatheories that attempt to provide monolithic explanations of power. For him there is only the **micropolitics** of power.

Q The **micropolitics** of power?

A Yes—how power is exercised in various local situations. The prison, the hospital, the asylum, the university, the bedroom are all places where power relationships are at work. Even S/M, for

espoused such local struggles.

But Baudrillard commands that we forget Foucault, because his ideas about power are obsolete.

Q **Why obsolete?**

A Because, according to Baudrillard, power is dead, dissolved, canceled and made hyperreal through **simulations, models, codes**.

In the new Postmodern universe of mediablitz, we no longer have power per se—but something Foucault forgot about—**simulations** of power. For instance, Ronald Reagan ruled like a king merely by **posing**—by offering **signs** of power in photo ops and sound bites—rather than by exercising power.

Foucault, is a kind of game, a way of exploring the dimensions of power locally. No grand general theory can explain how power works in all these sites.

Furthermore, everywhere there is power there is resistance. And the only way to resist power is locally—to resist localized practices of repression. Gays, feminists, former communists and other marginalized groups have

But if power is dead—so is sexuality!

According to Foucault sexuality refers to talk and writing about erotic practices, which contain rules and prohibitions and distinguish normal sex from perversions. But according to Baudrillard, in the new Postmodern era sex is dead because everything is sex. Sexual simulations are everywhere, in advertising, in fashion, on TV, in film. Sexuality is no longer intimate, personal and private behavior. It is open, encouraged, unlimited, unrestricted, mandatory—a command to release sexual tensions (built up through the sex-everywhere display of sexuality) through sexual codes. Thus "Everything is sexuality" (FF 14). But if *everything* is sexuality—then *nothing* is sexuality!

Jacques Derrida

Q **Well, if sex is dead in the Postmodern, Poststructural universe, then is there anything left? It seems that everything has been destroyed.**

A And that brings us to deconstruction—the brainchild of French-trained philosopher Jacques Derrida.

Weren't Foucault and Bau-
drillard French as well? Why is
so much Postmodern and Post-
structutralist thought dominated by French thinkers?

A Well France, during the
Enlightenment (the 18th century), as we have already
talked about, really invented
the idea of the intellectual—
the idea of a cerebral elite who
would sit back and just sort of
think about things. And from
the time of the Enlightenment, France has been a
kind of paradise for
intellectuals, a place
where philosophers and
thinkers have been regarded as
national treasures. Their books
are snapped up as readily as the
latest thriller, their disputes and
divagations are written up in
glossy, mass-media magazines,
they appear on TV talk shows,
they get good-looking lovers and
good seats at restaurants. In
exchange for these favors, they
are expected to set a moral tone,
to buck established values, and

most important—to be avant
garde. They rest secure in the
knowledge that what they think
today, the rest of France will be
thinking tomorrow. At times, their
wisdom even overspills French bor-
ders, flooding the greater intellectual world with French ideas.

For decades, on the sidewalks outside the cafes of Paris, light has danced down through the boughs along the boulevards, playing over the surfaces of objects, dappling tablecloths and variously attired torsos with swarms of ephemeral hues. French cafe-goers, many of them people of intelligence and culture, have placed orders, fumbled for cigarettes, and found it very attractive to be able to sit at a table and talk about the table and, raising an intellectual eyebrow in the dappled light, to ask if the table is.

Presiding over all this table talk, from the time of the French Revolution, the image of the philosopher was one of the intellectual engage,

who, besides wondering if the table is or is not, was to be found engaged in political and public affairs. In recent times, up until the late 1960s, Jean-Paul Sartre defined the image. But then the icon of the intellectual changed.

At the same time young Americans were tripping to Jimi Hendrix, "Hey Jude," Hair, and 2001: A Space Odysey, a student movement swept

across Europe. As we have already talked about, French students, supported by the Marxists, took to the streets, fighting the army and police in order to overthrow the government. They nearly succeeded, but were eventually quelled. Failing to demolish state power, they became disillusioned, inward-looking. Suddenly exhibiting a Postmodern scepticism about grand myths such as Marxism and Communism, they began to commit themselves to language itself. Disengaging themselves from politics, they became linguistic revolutionaries, finding revolution in turns of speech, and they began to view literature, reading and writing as subversive political acts in themselves.

deconstruction

French intellectuals began attending to **how** words say more than to **what** words

say. Increasingly distrustful of language claiming to convey only a single, authoritarian message, they began exploring **how** language can say many different things simultaneously. But by the time all this had taken place Jacques Derrida had emerged, in the late 1960s, as the most avant garde of the avant garde. His lecture given at the Johns Hopkins University in 1966, "**Structure, Sign and Play in the Discourse of the Human Sciences,**"

caused many previous philosophers to be reassessed, and it set the tone for much thought to come. It was something of a disharmonious chord, for his forte was a subversive mode of reading authoritarian texts, or any texts. This style of reading came to be known as *deconstruction*. In France, deconstruction, kicking existentialism aside, was suddenly much in vogue. Derrida became the philosopher of the day, the new enfant terrible of French intellectualism. And then, after the American debut at Johns Hopkins, deconstruction and Jacques Derrida took America by storm, turning much of the Western worldview topsy-turvy.

Q Well, tell me then, what is deconstruction?

A Defining deconstruction is an activity that goes against the whole thrust of Derrida's thought. Actually, Derrida has said that any statement such as "deconstruction is 'X'" automatically misses the point. But deconstruction often involves a way of reading that concerns itself with decentering—with unmasking the problematic nature of all centers.

Q Decentering? Centers? What is a center? What is problematic about one? Why should one need to be decentered?

A Well, Derrida, when he is not deconstructing a text of some difficult philosopher such as Nietzsche or Heidegger, writes about centers in such abstract language, that I will offer some concrete examples. According to Derrida, all Western thought is based on the idea of a center—an origin, a Truth, an Ideal Form, a Fixed Point, an Immovable Mover, an Essence, a God, a Presence,

which is usually capitalized, and which guarantees all meaning.

For instance, for 200 years, much of Western culture has been centered on the idea of Christianity and Christ. Other cultures, as well, all have their own central symbols.

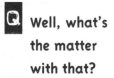 **Well, what's the matter with that?**

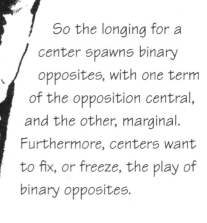

A The problem withcenters, for Derrida, is that they attempt to exclude. In doing so they ignore, repress or marginalize others (which become the Other). In male-dominated societies, man is central (and woman is the marginalized Other, repressed, ignored, pushed to the margins).

If you have a culture which has Christ in the center of its icons, then Christians will be central to that culture, and Buddhists, Muslims, Jews—anybody different—will be in the margins, marginalized, pushed to the outside. *(We must remember that Derrida was born into an assimilated Jewish family in Algiers, growing up as a member of a marginalized, dispossessed culture).*

So the longing for a center spawns binary opposites, with one term of the opposition central, and the other, marginal. Furthermore, centers want to fix, or freeze, the play of binary opposites.

Q Fix the play of binary opposites? What does that mean?

A Well, the opposition man/woman is just one binary opposite. Others are spirit/matter; nature/culture; Caucasian/Black; Eurocentrism/Afrocentrism; and Christian/pagan. According to Derrida we have no access to reality except through concepts, codes and categories, and the human mind functions by forming conceptual pairs such as these. You see how one member of the pair, (here the left), is privileged. The right-hand term then becomes marginalized. Icons with Christ or Buddha or whatever in the center try to tell us that what is in the center is the only reality. All other views are repressed. Drawing such an icon is an attempt to fix the play of opposites between, for example, Christian/Jew or Christian/pagan. The Jew and the pagan are not even represented in such art. But icons are just one of the social practices— there are many more— that try to fix the play of opposites— advertising, social codes, taboos, conventions, categories, rituals, etc. But reality and language are not as simple and singular as icons with a central, exclusive image in their middle—they are more like ambiguous figures.

The interesting thing about such figures is that at first we

see only one possibility. One possibility is "central" for a moment. For a moment the figure signifies faces, but then, because the play of the system is not arrested, the other view dawns, and the same figure signifies a candle.

But suppose a group seizes power, a group called the Face-ists (I have deliberately made this sound like "Fascists"). They might draw eyes on the faces. This would be an attempt to fix or arrest the free play of differences.

In such a situation, Candle-ists would be marginalized, repressed and even oppressed or persecuted. The image of the faces becomes the privileged member of the original pair. In other words, a violent hierarchy is formed in which the central-ized member of the pair, the face, becomes instituted as the Real and the Good.

Derrida says that all of Western thought behaves in this same way, forming pairs of bina-ry opposites in which one mem-ber of the pair is privileged,

freezing the play of the system, and marginalizing the other member of the pair. But the figure, in reality, signifies both faces and a candle.

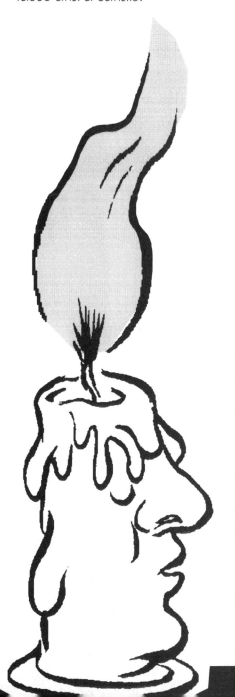

Q **Yes, but how does this apply to language, to literature, to reading?**

A Deconstruction is a tactic of decentering, a way of reading, which first reminds us of the centrality of the central term. Then it attempts to subvert the central term so that the marginalized term can become central. The marginalized term then temporarily overthrows the hierarchy.

Suppose you have a poem such as the following haiku:

And suppose that for thousands of years the only correct way of reading the poem is to read "pines" as a verb—like pining for one's lost love.

Q **O.K. But what about the other meaning? Can't "pines," in the context of the second line, switch over and become a noun: "Pines upon the mountainside?"**

A Yes, that's right. That would be the second move in deconstructing a piece of literature—to subvert the privileged term by revealing how the repressed, marginalized meaning can just as well be central.

Q But what good does that do? Doesn't this just institute a new center? Instead of "pines" the verb we have "pines" the noun. Or instead of Face-ists we now have Candle-ists in power?

A Exactly. Derrida claims that deconstruction is a political practice, and that one must not pass over and neutralize the phase of subversion too quickly. For this phase of reversal is needed in order to subvert the original hierarchy of the first term over the second. But eventually, one must realize that this new hierarchy is equally unstable, and surrender to the complete free-play of the binary opposites in a non-hierarchical way. Then you can see that both readings, and many others, are equally possible.

Q Yes! Like "pines upon the mountain sighed" (instead of "mountainside")!

A So you can see the possibilities. If the text were the Communist Manifesto or the Torah or the Koran or the Bible or the Constitution, you could deconstruct any fixed, authoritarian, dogmatic, or orthodox reading. Of course, such texts are much more complex than our haiku. They are more multifaceted, like the drawing below.

If you have a system of triangles such as this, then you will notice that if you stare at it, a series of configurations of triangles **presents** itself to your vision—one after the other. But each so-called **present** configuration, each group of triangles which seems to be momentarily **present**, has emerged out of a prior configuration and is already dissolving into a future configuration. And this play goes on endlessly. There is no central configuration that attempts to freeze the play of the system, no marginal one, no privileged one, no repressed one. According to Derrida all language and all texts are, when deconstructed, like this. And so is human thought, which is always made up of language. He says we should continuously attempt to see this free play in all our language and texts—which otherwise will tend toward fixity, institutionalization, centralization, totalitarianism, exclusion. For in our **anxiety** we always feel a need to construct new centers, to associate ourselves with them, and to marginalize those who are different than their central values.

Q I see, then. Deconstruction first focuses on the binary oppositions within a text—like man/woman. Next it shows how these opposites are related, how one is regarded as central, natural and privileged—the other ignored, repressed and marginalized. Next it temporarily undoes, subverts or decenters the hierarchy to make the text mean the opposite of what it originally appeared to mean. Then, in the last step, both terms of the opposition are deconstructed—seen dancing in a free play of nonhierarchical, non-stable meanings. But if language is just the free play of meanings—with no fixed meanings—if all texts degenerate into the play of meanings, then there is no basis for political action.

A That's right. In fact, many Marxists and feminists have attacked deconstruction because it cannot provide a firm foundation for political action or even political criticism.

Q **And if language is fragmented, then people, who use language, must be somewhat fragmented too.**

A Yes, this is what many Postmodernists theorize. Whereas the mental diseases of modernism were alienation and paranoia, schizophrenia is the Postmodern mental disease. If the sentence breaks down, so does the psyche. So does our experience of past, present and future. Thus Postmodernism wallows in the play of meanings, it surfs these meanings and is concerned with performance, play and process rather than with the finished product. Postmodernism delights in the ever-changing play of appearances, rather than with sources and roots and origins. Which gets us to our next Poststructuralists, Deleuze and Guattari, whose idea of the rhizome is opposed to the root.

Deleuze and Guattari

Gilles Deleuze and Felix Guattari are two French Poststructuralists who have had a major impact on American thought.

> ### THEY BELIEVE, QUITE SIMPLY, THAT WE SHOULD STOP BELIEVING IN TREES AND ROOTS.

For, according to them, most of Western thought is dominated by a structure of knowledge they call **aborescence**. The way of knowing is tree-like, vertical. For instance, in biology we have Linnaean taxonomies.

In chemistry we have Porphyrian trees:

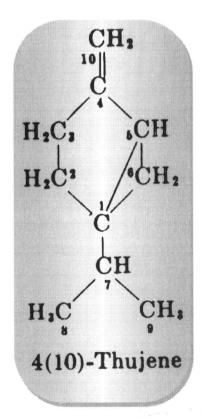

4(10)-Thujene

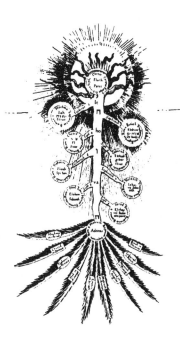

```
                              S
              NP ───────────────────         VP
           ╱   │   ╲                        ╱    ╲
          a   man   S                      is   honest
                  ╱   ╲
                NP     VP
                │     ╱  ╲
               man   is   wise
```

Such trees show up not only in the fields of biology, botany, linguistics and anatomy, but also in philosophy—where we have metaphysical trees, theological trees, gnostic trees, The World Tree, genealogical trees.

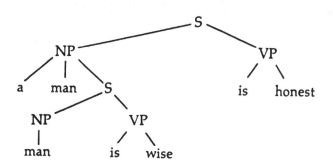

These trees are hierarchical, imposing limited and regulated connections between their components.

All such trees spread out like many branches and stems from a single trunk—each steming from an original oneness or unity.

MAMA

tree-like because all the various psychic processes can be traced back to an original traumatic event in which the child is separated from the mother. This lack of the mother is the basis of desire, and is compensated for only by the child's entry into the symbolic order—the order of Law and the Name-of-the-Father.

Of course, all this can be traced back to Plato, whose vertical, tree-like philosophy proclaimed a material world of manifestations stemming from the "trunk" of a realm of Ideal Forms or Essences.

For instance, Doberman Pinschers, German shepherds, collies and poodles are all material manifestations of an immaterial Essence—an Ideal Form of what Plato might call Dogginess.

Dogginess is the single Platonic Origin—the Trunk—of the tree of dogs. Poodles, collies, etc. form the branches.

A major tree-like structure that Deleuze and Guattari criticize is the Oedipus complex. It is

But Deleuze and Guattari reject the idea of the Oedipus triangle—of the father-principle, and of desire based on lack. Desire, for Deleuze and Guattari, instead of being based on lack and

OH, YEAH, JUST SPELL MY NAME BACKWARDS.

rooted in an original Oedipal trauma, is created horizontally, by social interconnections. And the interconnections between the infant and his surrounding society are always in movement, flowing, taking lines of flight, like a stringer of crabgrass … like a rhizome.

So, opposed to the vertical, tree-like structure of knowledge, Deleuze and Guattari proclaim a rhizomatic, radically horizontal, crabgrass-like way of knowing. Crabgrass, for instance, is a plant. But instead of one central root, it has zillions of roots, none of which is central—and each offshoot interconnects in random, unregulated networks in which any node can interconnect with any other node.

Whereas the tree seeks to establish itself and say "to be," the rhizome is always rearranging interconnections, saying "and, and, and, and …"

Thus the tree is concerned with origins, foundations, ontologies, beginnings and endings—roots. The rhizome is concerned with surface connections, lines of flight, with the "and."

According to Deleuze and Guattari, the works of the writer Franz Kafka are rhizomatic—interconnected like a maze of rat tunnels. Much of Kafka's work is like a nightmare. But the images and symbols of his dreamlike literature do not mean anything. They do not represent anything. For this would entail a tree-like structure of knowledge—a vertical structure connecting the meaning and the images and symbols representing the meaning. So dream symbols do not mean anything or represent anything. They are not there to be interpreted.

It is good enough merely to describe dreams and, in doing so to watch how their symbols open up new, horizontal interconnections between other symbols.

For instance, in Kafka's "Letter to His Father" he inflates his father to laughably absurd, dreamlike dimensions, until his father's singular Fatherness gets so huge that it pops—exploding into a vast rhizomatic network of father-like social connections represented by judges, commissioners, bureaucrats. In this way, Kafka laughs the Father—and the Oedipal structure—out of existence.

In Kafka's short story, **_The Metamorphosis_,** the main character, Gregor Samsa, awakes one morning only to find that he has been transformed into a huge bug. Some critics regard the relationship between Gregor and his mother and father as typically Oedipal. But again, Kafka explodes the Father's single image into many, including a chief clerk and a boss. Kafka thus tries to de-Oedipalize Gregor's father. But in the end Gregor's line of flight fails, and like a good son, he dies for his family.

It is only in Kafka's novels that the rhizomatic line of flight truly succeeds—especially in **The Trial**. One might expect a novel named The Trial to have something to do with the law. But Deleuze and Guattari find that Justice in the novel is not legal but erotic. Justice is really desire. Thus, there are obscene drawings in the courthouse; an attorney equates being accused with being attractive; a series of suggestive encounters with sexy, antifamilial women; and a painting of Justice as winged, and evasive. K., the protagonist of the novel, never reaches Justice. "She" is never present, but always one room away from him in the rhizomatic, rat tunnel of the courthouse with its crazy corridors and perversely connected passageways through which K. is led by eroticized women. Thus Justice, like the courthouse and desire, is rhizomatic, never reaching conclusion. Kafka's writing, too, is rhizomatic, mapping and toying with the structures of institutions and social relations.

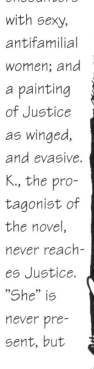

A Yes. It is non-hierarchical, horizontal. Its nodes intersect in random, unregulated networks in which any node can interconnect with any other node. In this respect Deleuze and Guattari were correct when they declared a new form of rhizomatic, horizontal knowledge. In fact, there is a story in the March 18, 1996 *New Yorker* entitled "Virtual Bishop."

The bishop indicated is Jacques Guillot, who was exiled by the Vatican to Algeria for his "heterodox" opinions. Stuck in the middle of the desert—in an ancient diocese that for all practical purposes no longer exists—he went online, becoming the world's first virtual bishop.

It was a visionary author, Leo Scheer, who hooked up the bishop. He is quoted as saying that "*Instead of a metaphysical idea of a bishop, attached to a real place, we would have a metaphysical idea of a place, attached to a real bishop.*"

The virtual diocese, which can be accessed from anywhere in the world, imitates the mind of God—a horizontal, rhizomatic God. In fact, the bishop, who counts among his friends people like Jean Baudrillard, complains that until the opening of the virtual diocese, "*The Church has been organized vertically, when we ought to be organized horizontally.*" Of course, the Church soon went online as well.

Q It seems like vertical is out and horizontaL is in.

A Yes, but the ironic thing is HOW, in 1995, Deleuze committed suicide.

David Harvey

The Condition of Postmodernity

Q **It seems as if his self must have been pretty fragmented. But where does the fragmentation—of language, of the self, and of "things"—common to both modernism and Postmodernism come From?**

A Well, according to David Harvey's **The Condition of Postmodernity**, fragmentation in the arts, language, and the human psyche has come about through a change in the way time and space are perceived.

Postmodernism has been influenced by dramatic differences in the way we experience space and time. And whenever significant changes in our perception of time and space occur, this brings about equally large changes in the ways we represent the world—both in the arts and in philosophy.

The history of capitalism has brought on what Harvey calls space-time compression: There has been an increase in the pace of life. And paralleling the increasing compression in time, space has shrunk. The world seems to collapse inwards on us.

But it was not always like this. During Europe's feudal era, each feudal fiefdom was a definite legal, political, economic and social world. At the center was the castle, the Lord and Lady of the castle and the nobility. Working the fields and the forests, a class of serfs were loyal to their feudal lords. Of course, this feudal world was thought to be only a reflection of a cosmos ruled on high by God and a gang of heavenly hosts, and populated by darker characters, the creatures of myth and folklore—witches, giants, dragons.

Medieval mapmakers often represented this world in sensuous detail, almost like a painting. In such maps, a river is a sensuous flow of blue paint that cuts through a dark forest (represented by painting in a number of trees)—and beyond we find the castle. A cross shining from the steeple of the church and its surrounding buildings are also all represented as they might be in a painting. These details are see from a bird's-eye perspective, as if God were looking down upon the scene. At the edge of such maps was the end of the world—and a cosmic dragon waiting to swallow anyone who would dare venture too close to the edge and fall into his mouth.

With the Renaissance, the principle of perspective made its appearance. Perspectivism shifted the angle of vision from God to that of an individual human being free of the naive superstitions of myth and religion. At the same time, the Ptolemaic system of mapmaking made its way to Europe—a system that represented space objectively. From then on, a mathematical grid—a geometric framework allowing viewers to actually measure distances between towns and oceans—would appear on all maps. Now, since all of space, all of the world, could be represented by a geometric grid, the whole globe was suddenly knowable and conquerable. Explorers, setting out on voyages of discovery, drew such maps, which were then valuable to merchants and traders.

At the same time that space became chopped up mathematically, the clock, or chronometer, made its appearance.

These new conceptions of space and time were reflected in every sphere of Renaissance culture. In architecture, Gothic cathedrals had been populated with grotesque gargoyles and angels. But these gave way, in the Baroque era, to a more expansive architecture, to the soaring energies of Bach's fugues and the expansive images of space and time in John Donne's poetry. But this new, infinite, measured image of time and space still reflected God's glory.

Then the 18th-century Enlightenment saw space as something to be conquered. Maps were purged of all elements of fantasy and religion and became abstract, geometric, cold, mathematical, and strictly functional.

Both time and space became uniform, mechanical, Newtonian space and time. But if the whole world could be envisioned as uniform, if land could be laid out on a grid and divided up equally—as was done in the United States—then this could create the

brated God's infinite glory but displayed the dimensions of a universe that could be dominated by MAN. And used by Man for his own freedom. No longer would one fear falling off the edge of the earth into the mouth of a cosmic monster.

Europeans thought that now there was a place in this conquerable space for everyone. Africa could provide slaves, and other continents and climes could provide raw materials for the imperial European and American powers.

The chronometer allowed time, like space, to be seen as mathematical and uniform. Time now ticked away in a straight line from the past to the future.

basis for equality in society. It could create the basis for democracy.

In other words, the view of a rational, uniform grid of space and time allowed Enlightenment thinkers to envision colonial and utopian plans that could be rolled out over the whole uniform grid of the globe. Space was knowable, and through Euclidean geometry, conquerable. Space, nature, and the world could be measured, known and dominated.

For Enlightenment thinkers this vast grid of space and time no longer cele-

Modernism saw the breaking up of these uniform, linear, conceptions of space and time. During the Enlightenment social time and physical time had merged, had become uniform and mathematical. Time had become progressive.

But in the mid-nineteenth century, this progressive sense of time was shaken. Many Europeans who had participated in uprisings and revolutions had had a taste of explosive time. Those caught up in class struggles had a sense of alternating, cyclic time.

Also, by the mid-nineteenth century, it became evident that economic and social time had changed. With improvements in transportation and communications, all of Europe was becoming economically interdependent. If Paris should suffer a financial crisis, the crisis also affected London and Berlin.

Similarly, workers in various countries began to sympathize with each other, and in such an environment, the Communist Manifesto, could gain an audience.

After 1850, the major European nations expanded globally, stripping much of the space in the world of its previous names and uses. It became routine for nations, cities and individuals to be deeply influenced by events thousands of miles away. The radio, the motor car, and the train accelerated these developments.

How could any writer, then, still write a realistic novel with a plot unfolding page after page in simple, step-by-step, chronological order?

Writers such as Flaubert, Proust and James Joyce began to capture this sense of simultaneous time by altering the structures of their plots.

Einstein's revolutionary theories of relativity changed the perception of space and time even more. Impressionist painters such as  Manet and Cezanne began to decompose the space of objects within paintings—objects dissolving into dabs of light. Cubism further decomposed the object. In sociology Durkheim's **Elementary Forms of Religious Life**, published in 1912, founded the sense of time in social rhythms. It became apparent that there are as many experiences of space and time as there are perspectives.

Now, in the Postmodern world, the shrinking of space has changed the ways that money and commodities operate. Capital is now electronically moved around the global marketplace with such rapidity that it has lost much of its stability and meaning. In our local supermarkets, we can buy French cheeses and wines, beers from Canada, Mexico, Asia and Europe, green beans from South America or Africa, Tahitian mangoes, California celery, Canadian apples, etc. Space is also compressed in the populations of the largest cities, increasingly made up of minorities such as Vietnamese, Koreans, Eastern Europeans, Central Americans, Africans, etc.

Postmodern Artifacts

As space shrinks more and more, the individual qualities of different spaces, different localities, grows in importance. Certain provinces in France become very important if they can provide a certain kind of wine or cheese. Certain Pacific Rim nations become important if they can provide inexpensive labor. World capital must be flexible in order to exploit all these labor and commodity markets—must move around the globe quickly, taking advantage of various niches. This is flexible accumulation, as opposed to the fixed accumulation of the early 20th century, when corporations like Ford Motor Company and their capital basically sat in one place and pumped out cars for a relatively stable market.

Harvey believes that the ephemerality, collage and fragmentation of Postmodern artifacts such as books, films, architecture and art are simply mirrors of this phenomenon of flexible accumulation.

Blade Runner

An example of this is the movie Bladerunner, which contains significant Postmodern elements.

"Blade Runner" is a Victorian word for "private eye." The film became a cult film––and then a kind of national specimen of Postmodernism. It even

inspired William Gibson's novel **Neuromancer** and the movement that has come to be known as <u>cyberpunk</u>.

Blade Runner is about a gang of genetically produced humans called "replicants" who have been created to serve as hyper-strong, intelligent and skilled slaves. The are used "off-world," in the hazardous work of exploring and colonizing the outer planets.

Although they have been given human emotions, they are considered somewhat dangerous, and as part of their genetic program, have a life span of only four years.

Q **It looks as if they would be good short-contract workers in a Postmodern world. But are they human beings or not?**

A Do you remember Jean Baudrillard's concept of the simulacrum?

Q **Sure, the simulacrum is the copy that is so close to the original that the original is no longer important.**

A And that's what replicants have become—simulacra that are nearly indistinguishable from human beings. In fact *Blade Runner* portrays a Baudrillardian world in which "*The real is produced from miniaturized units, from matrices, memory banks and command modules—and with these it can be reproduced an indefinite number of times*" (SIM 3).

And the replicants have returned to Los Angeles, where they were made, in order to meet their maker, a genetic designer named Tyrell, who is the head of the huge Tyrell Corporation, and is in command of the reproductive processes necessary for creation of replicants. The replicants are angry about their short life span. However, Tyrell explains to Roy, the leader of the enraged replicants, that they should enjoy their short life because it is more intense—like a flame that burns twice as brightly but has only a short duration.

Q **But doesn't that make them like the Postmodern personalities—caught up in the rush of time?**

A Yes. And the Los Angeles they return to, supposedly Los Angeles of the year 2019, is no utopia. In fact it is a dystopia, a decayed, Post-industrial wasteland.

On the lowest level,

empty warehouses and industrial plants lie half-buried in heaps of rotting rubbish, which are scavenged by roaming bands of punks and other human vultures living on the decaying remains of the past.

On the middle level,

the bustle of street life, it looks something like Hong Kong (on a bad day) crowded with punks, various riff-raff, Hare Krishna devotees, and other marginal street folk.

On the highest level,

soaring high above the street scum, towers a high-tech world of corporate power, architecture and advertising: Pan Am, Coca Cola, Budweiser. But hovering above all the corporate offices is the Tyrell Corporation itself.

Not only the replicants are simulacra, but the architecture of the city is too. It is an eclectic Postmodern hodgepodge of simulacra. The Tyrell corporate headquarters looks like a replica, a simulacrum of a pyramid, lost among a bazaar of Greek, Roman, Mayan, Chinese, and Victorian motifs.

The profusion of corporate architecture and advertising signs in the city, which combines elements of New York, Tokyo, Hong Kong and Los Angeles, is nothing so much as a chaos of circulating signs referring to other signs.

The PAST is NOW

The Postmodern artistic principle at work here is pastiche, a series of neutral quotations mimicking various architectural styles and film styles. Everything is double coded.

Q What is double coding, again?

A You will remember that in architecture double coding consists of using Modernist methods, but transcending them by simultaneously quoting architectural motifs from the past or from a local culture—but consciously, in a playful, pastiche-sort of way that can be humorous or ironic.

Q Like the AT&T building that is at once a piece of modern architecture and a quote of a grandfather clock?

A Yes. And double coding can occur not only in architecture but in just about any art form. So in **Blade Runner**, everything is double coded. There are not only human replicants; **everything** is a replicant. The actors replicate an eclectic blend of movie genres and period styles—for **Blade Runner**

is both a futuristic film, set 40 years in the future (from the 1980s) and set simultaneously 40 years in the past—it quotes extensively from the genre of noir films of the 1940s. Some of the sets are actually sets from old Bogart and James Cagney movies. Architecturally, everything is quoted also: Frank Lloyd Wright, Greek and Roman columns, along with Oriental motifs and 40s gangster set themes. Thus the motive is not parody but play— pastiche. It is the surface play and display of the simulacra. Just as the replicants are more human than humans, the simulacra have become more real than the real.

In fact, a main question of the film is, What is the difference between a machine and a human being? Replicants and human beings are so much alike that it is very difficult to tell the copy from the "real thing." What is the difference between a human being and a Nexus-6 android? What is the difference between an original and a simulacrum?

This question is brought to a head in the relationship between Rick Deckard—a private eye who has been hired by the Tyrell Corporation to act as a search-and-destroy agent in pursuit of Nexus-6 replicants—and Rachel, a beautiful brunette replicant with whom he falls in love. She does not know whether she is a replicant or not. This causes Deckard to doubt his own human history. After he kills one of her fellow androids, Rachael is visibly disturbed. Deckard says "Replicants weren't supposed to have feelings, but then again, nor were Blade Runners."

At another point Decker and Rachel, human and android, are about to sleep together. Rachel says, "You're not going to bed with a woman.... Remember, though, don't think about it, just do it. Don't pause and be philosophical, because from a philosophical standpoint it's dreary for us both."

But the movie does make us think about it philosophically. In fact, much of Postmodern art is just a way of thinking about the Postmodern age. It is a way of doing Postmodern theory. And after all, the movie spawned the whole movement of **cyberpunk**, a movement that dramatizes the growing concern with the relationship between human beings and computers.

Q Could this, then, be another difference between modernism and Postmodernism?

A How's that?

Cyborgs

Q Well, one of the central images modernists used to fill in the post-Nietzschian void was that of the machine. Perhaps Postmodernism has just replaced the image of the simple machine with that of the Man-machine—the hybrid of man and machine.

A Actually, that's exactly what Donna Haraway declares in another important Post-modern essay, "A Cyborg Manifesto: Science, Technology, and Socialist Formation in the Late Twentieth Century." This essay is actually a chapter in her book *Simians, Cyborgs and Women: The Reinvention of Nature.*

Q   Well, what's a cyborg?

A   A cyborg is a cybernetic organism. Half

human, half comput-er. Haraway argues that in the late twentieth century, and probably for some time to come, we are all cyborgs.

Q   But are we all cyborgs? I don't have any machine parts.

A   Haraway uses "cyborg" to construct a new myth about being human. Old

myths about being human always go back to some idyllic time of wholeness and unity and inno-cence, like in the Garden of Eden. But the myth of the cyborg is never about wholes; it does not look nostalgically back to some unified origin. A cyborg is always a split, a hybrid identity, a cybernetic organism: a human-computer.

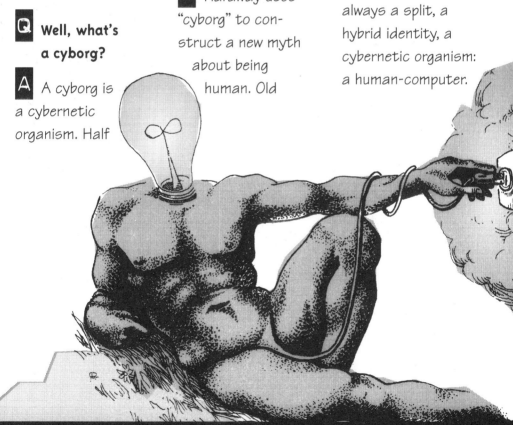

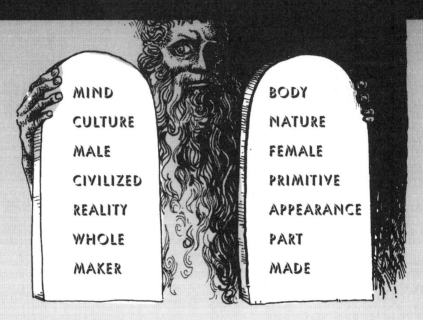

MIND	BODY
CULTURE	NATURE
MALE	FEMALE
CIVILIZED	PRIMITIVE
REALITY	APPEARANCE
WHOLE	PART
MAKER	MADE

For in our culture, we always try to favor the words on the left and repress the ones on the right. But if we see ourselves as cyborgs, then we can know that we are always both: mind and body, culture and nature, male and female, etc.—fractured identities, human-computers. And, in a way, we are. Every Asian woman who, with her nimble fingers, works in the electronics industry, assembling computers, every secretary whose typing speed is monitored on the computer by her boss, every check-out clerk at the grocery store whose speed is calculated by a computer, every voter, every consumer is being monitored by a computer—is part of a computer—is a cybernetic organism. It is hard to tell where the computer stops and the organism begins.

Q **Well, why don't these workers just rebel?**

A That's one of the sentiments that gave rise to the whole cyberpunk movement.

130

Cyberpunk

Q Cyberpunk?

A Yes. Cyberpunk was once considered the most Postmodern of all Postmodern things. Cyberpunk began as a hybrid of 80s counterculture, cybertechnology and anarchy.

The "cyber" part of cyberpunk indicates that, like cyborg, it has something to do with computers.

The word "punk" gives us a clue to the attitude that cyberpunks have toward computer technology: hip, sexy, violent, mind-altered, anti-authoritarian, rebellious, with a distaste for the dominant lifestyles of the Reagan/Bush era.

Real-life cyberpunks tend to operate somewhat outside the law, as they are opposed to the centralized use of computer technologies by huge megacorporations and states. They are often hackers who use cybertechnology to tap into the international electronic grid to fulfill their own individual desires. A cyberpunk guy who wants to seduce some corporate secretary might soften her up by softening up her softwear (e.g., by altering the software in the corporate mainframe so that it appears to her boss—who monitors her key stroke rate—that she is typing twice as fast as she actually is).

Cyberpunks, unlike hippies, are not against technology. They want to use technology as a means to resist the infringement on our individual freedoms by centralized techno-giants.

Just as Mary Shelley's *Frankenstein* warned against the excesses and dangers of the industrial and scientific revolution in the 19th century, science fiction writing that goes by the name of cyberpunk warns of a techno-future in which humans must fight against the technological powers of giant international megacorporations. But that technological future is now!

Neuromancer

The first cyberpunk novel, which was inspired, in part, by *Blade Runner*, is William Gibson's *Neuromancer*. The story is about Case, a petty computer and data thief who has stolen information from his bosses. As punishment, his nerve cells have been burned out.

Case's nervous system is repaired, however, when he is hired by a mysterious employer to perform a Big Heist. He is accompanied by some hired muscle in the form of Molly, a gal brimming with bio-implants, including razors beneath her nails. Together they steal a computer construct.

The major adventure in the novel is their mission to Freeland, a planet where they are to steal an Artificial Intelligence entity named Necromancer with whom Wintermate (the mysterious employer) wishes to merge so that he may become God and take over the universe.

The difference between *Blade Runner* and *Neuromancer* is that in *Neuromancer* the difference between computer and human, nature and technology, original and copy, original and simulacrum, has collapsed—imploded. In fact, *Neuromancer* starts out with a description of nature that is in terms of technology: "The sky above the port was the color of television, tuned to a dead channel" (N 3).

133

And it is Case's own repaired nervous system, for instance, not some computer, which enables him to enter cyberspace.

And though everyone today knows what cyberspace is, Gibson was the one who invented the term. He did so by saying that cyberspace is: "**A consensual hallucination experienced daily by billions of legitimate operators in every nation...a graphic representation of data abstracted from the banks of every computer in the human system. Unthinkable complexity. Lines of light ranged in the nonspace of the mind, clusters of constellations of data. Like city lights receding**" (N 51).

Cyberspace is a cyborg—a merging of human and computer capacities. And this concept of cyberspace was suggested to Gibson one day in Vancouver, as he was watching some teenagers playing video games in an arcade:

"I could see in the physical intensity of their postures how rapt these kids were.... You had this feedback loop, with photons coming off the screen into the kids' eyes, the neurons moving through their bodies, electrons moving through the computer. And those kids clearly believed in the space these games projected."

Teledidonics, Audio-animatronic Paparazzi & Nano-Rovers

Cyberpunk science fiction is not so much about the future as it is a way of drawing a map of what is going on today—a present in which data are controlled by vast technocapitalistic corporations. But these huge data banks exist in a space where TV, telex, tape recorder, VCR, laser

OH, BABY...

disk, camcorder, teledildo, audioanimatronic paparazzi, nano-rover and telephone are wired together like a sprawling electronic species of cosmic crab-grass. And they can be plugged into by those with the hacker, cybperpunk ethic of "information for the people."

Q **Teledildo? Audioanimatronic paparazzi? Nano-rover? What are those?**

A **Teledildonics** involves a kind of computer sex in which a joy-stick-dildo can be animated by a user on a distant computer. **Audioanimatronic paparazzi** are sound-activated robotic paparazzi which snap your photo

(as if you were a super-model strutting in thigh-highs into a glitzy theme restaurant such as the Fashion Cafe, or) while engaged in noisy teledildonics with someone of National-Enquirer-front-cover status—someone such as a distant Martian. A **nano-rover** is an impossibly small robotic that sends back pixel images from the surface of Mars. And so you can see the possibilities: the data from teledildo, Martian, nano-rover and audio-animatronic paparazzi—all interacting in one huge cosmic electronic event.

Q Cyberpunk science fiction seems to provide a more accurate map of the contours of these Postmodern times than does Baudrillard's theory.

A That's right. In fact, many think that Baudrillard is really doing science fiction, and that much of cyberpunk science fiction is really pretty good theory. After all, Baudrillard only describes a Postmodern society that passively surrenders to the sensual, obscene flow of hyperreality and simulacra. But cyberpunk science fiction not only describes a world of simulacra but also shows it to be a world dominated by vast mega-corporations, and suggests a form of resistance to the control these huge corporations exercise over us.

However, cyberpunk, like Baudrillard, has now ceased to be avant garde and is now merely hip.

Cyberpunk zines have become mainstream. *MONDO 2000*, a glossy cyber-glam zine, late '80s creation of R.U. Sirius and Queen Mu "domineditrix," is stuffed with rap on smart drugs, cyberfashion (cyberpunks often wear mirrorshades), cyber-gossip, etc.

Mondo's popularity was eclipsed, in 1993, by **Wired**, a site for cyberpunk authors such as William Gibson. **Wired** went online in 1994 as **HotWired**.

Web Hotwired
www.wired.com

Besides these popular magazines, tons of cyberpunk sci-fi has been pumped out. But it all sounds petty much the same. As Csicsery-Ronay asks:

"How many formulaic tales can one wade through in which a self-destructive but sensitive young protagonist with an (implant/prosthesis/telechtronic talent) that makes the evil (megacorporations/police states/criminal underworlds) pursue him through (wasted urban landscapes/elite luxury enclaves/eccentric space stations) full of grotesque (haircuts/clothes/self-mutilations/rock music/sexual hobbies/designer drugs/telechtronic gadgets/nasty new weapons/exteriorized hallucinations) representing the (mores/fashions) of modern civilization in terminal decline ultimately hooks up with rebellious and tough-talking (youth/artificial intelligence/rock cults) who offer the alternative, not of (community/socialism/traditional values/transcendental vision), but of supreme, life affirming *hippness*, going with the flow which now flows in the machine, against the specter of a world-subverting (artificial intelligence/multinational corporate web/evil genius)?"

(SRS 184)

137

Q Well, cyberpunk just sounds like a bunch of boys with high-tech power fantasies. How are these any different from Rambo? And what does cyberpunk have to say about the problems of crime, drug addiction, sex addiction, about women, about ecology?

A Whatever replaces cyberpunk will have to be more earth-centered and more woman-centered.

Madonna

Q WHat's so Postmodern about Madonna?

A Well, for one thing, she is quite consciously all surface, all put-on, all dress-up, all make-over, all simulation, all simulacrum. She knows that we live in an age of hype, of hyper-reality. She knows that simulation and appearance mean more than substance and reality. She knows that the appropriation and replication of the original are more real than the original. Thus she is deliberately trivial, shallow, formulaic. And not only in her videos. She realizes that "real" life is just show biz also. Thus she collects her paycheck but never really goes to work. When she dresses up as Marilyn Monroe she does so with the knowledge that Marilyn Monroe, herself, was just a put-on, a construction, a simulacrum, just like dressing up in drag or vogueing. Thus her dressing up as Marilyn Monroe is double coded in the same sense that *Blade Runner* and Postmodern architecture are double coded.

Some of her critics, people like feminists, teachers, Planned Parenthood, Veterans of Foreign Wars, etc. regard Madonna as just a cheesecakey whore dressed up in trashy junk jewelry, with a hi-there belly button and a fondle-my-bra, boy-toy attitude.

MORE WOMAN-CENTERED? LIKE MOI. HEY, I'M A REAL POMO MOMO.

Some Madonna-ologists, on the other hand, regard Madonna as deconstructing essentialist notions of male/female, high art/pop art, black/white, virgin/whore, fucker/fuckee, etc.

Q **Deconstructing essentialist notion of what?**

A Traditional gender roles, ideas of what it takes to be masculine or feminine, are kept in place by fixed polarities—binary opposites of sexual difference. For instance, it is supposedly a feminine game, not a masculine game, to wear a black-lace bra, with a little bit of strap showing at the shoulder. But in Madonna's videos men have breasts and wear bras, implying that they have breast envy (instead of the women having penis-envy), women have hard-ons, virgins are whores, and sluts are virgins.

"Displacement is at the core of the video's transgression where bodies intersect in the infamous bedroom scene. Multiple bodies shift positions in a series of displacements, while camera movement simulates the fluidity of erotic activity as it ranges over bodies, undisturbed by substitutions. Core identities surrender to the assumption of erotic roles in a splitting between dark and light, male and female, gay and straight—differences multiplied and compounded" (MPF 138-9).

By deconstructing the rigid boundaries between masculine and feminine, man and woman, gay and straight, Madonna's video *Justify My Love* has become a kind of gay anthem. It blurs the difference between sexual orientations, between gender and sex, portraying an erotic flow of fractured images that refuse to play either the lesbian or the hetero-sex 140 140 ual game, either the straight game or the gay game, either the black game or the white game, either the male game or the female game, but, with a little imagination and cross-dressing, plays the hybrid, mutant, hyperreal, lesbian-heterosexual game, the heterosexual-lesbian game, the mulatto-male-lesbian game, the half-breed-female-gay-man game.

Q But if Madonna's videos decontruct gender, sexuality and race, don't these videos—and the whole Madonna phenomenon—have something to do with power?

A Yes. Or with power fantasies. Natually, the powerless like power. And a large part of Madonna's power derives from her ability to produce images of rebelling against established powers. But, often the only power Madonna fans have is to buy her products: to increase the wealth of the multinational entertainment corporations that have them hypnotized.

Untitled Film Stills (Cindy Sherman)

Q **Hypnotized them?**

A Yes. The flow of media images hypnotizes and conditions us. The hyperreality of Madonna images becomes more real than the Madonna wanna-bes who imitate her. And this phenomenon—of the image being more real than the human—is dramatized by photographer Cindy Sherman in a series of photographs taken between 1977 and 1980 entitled **Untitled Film Stills**. The images are actually all of Cindy Sherman, the photographer, herself. But we do not see Cindy Sherman. What we see are images that appear in our mind's eye. These images act

something like masks, concealing "Cindy's" face (which is not so familiar to us) but reminding us of something familiar (yet, something we cannot quite grasp).

What we see, then, is not Cindy Sherman, but an image of a passed-out starlet, a hitch-hiker, a woman

opening a letter, etc. All of these images **seem** strangely familiar. But this is only because they were inspired, in part, by clichés from old Brigitte Bardot and Sophia Loren movies.

When you see one of her photos, you **think** you recognize a character or scene from an old movie you have seen. But, in fact, the photos do not reproduce any **specific** scenes in any movies but pull up in our **mind's eye** the **kinds** of visual **clichés** and **roles** women have played in old movies we have seen.

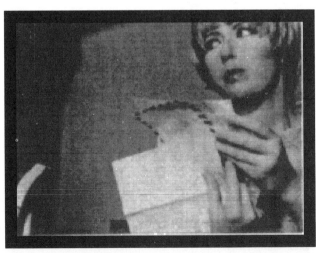

Thus, our moment of recognition is only an illusion. Though these images seem to refer to something other than themselves, they are all surface, all depthlessness.

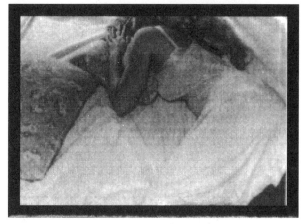

 MTV

Another Postmodern artifact is MTV.

Q **Why MTV?**

A Well, television, in general, is considered to be Postmodern because it is like a tornado of images that whirl by with such velocity that they have been stripped of all meaning—referring only to other images—the audience having reached the point of total saturation as the meaningless images glow and flicker, making the viewer into a kind of mindscreen.

Barbie-Art

Q **But some of the images *do* make sense. Most of the sit-coms and soaps have stories—narratives.**

A And that's why MTV is considered to be *especially* Postmodern. Because for most of TV, **storytelling—narrative**—has been the **norm**. But MTV is not based on stories but on **disconnected flows of images**. Then there is **subvertising**, a way of subverting the advertising campaigns of huge corporations by creating parodies of their messages, such as: "American Excess: Don't Leave Home Without It." This is closely associated with Barbie-art, the art of subverting Barbie-ism by placing Barbie dolls in compromising positions, dressing them up in boy's clothing, or, as the Barbie Liberation Organization did, switching the voice-boxes of Barbie dolls with those of G.I. Joe.

Q **What makes a novel or a film Postmodern?**

A Modernist novels concern themselves with the limits of individual consciousness— how the individual knows the world. In novels such as James Joyce's ***Portrait of the Artist as a Young Man***, the reader is plunged into the stream of thoughts and feelings of a young man as he attempts to know the world around him.

> THERE'S PROVIDENCE—
> SEND ME AN EAR
> WHEN IT'S CLEARLY
> AN EYE I NEED.

In the Postmodern novel or film, however, the question is not so much How do I know the world? but, What is a world?

Blue Velvet

Consider the film **Blue Velvet**, for example. It juxtaposes two very different worlds: a world of small-town, middle-class high school romance, and a world of murder and sadistic sexuality. It juxtaposes them in such a way that we do not know which world is more real.

Wings of Desire

Another film that is often branded "Postmodern" is Wim Wenders's **Wings of Desire**. Again, the film juxtaposes two very different worlds. The place is Berlin—international, cosmopolitan, filled with different languages and cultures and identities. Each of these is fragmented and isolated from the others. Each man lives in his own private world.

WE ARE CAPABLE OF LISTENING IN ON PEOPLE'S THOUGHTS:
TO A YOUNG MAN CONTEMPLATING SUICIDE; TO A DYING
MAN ON THE STREET; TO PEOPLE COMMUTING IN CARS; TO
MOTHERS AND FATHERS, LOVERS AND CHILDREN. EVERY
ALIENATED, ISOLATED INDIVIDUAL HAS BECOME LIKE A
LITTLE STATE WHERE EACH STREET HAS BARRIERS, AND ALL
IS SURROUNDED BY A NO-MAN'S LAND THROUGH WHICH ONE
CAN PASS ONLY IF ONE HAS THE RIGHT PASSWORD.

THE OTHER WORLD, JUXTAPOSED WITH A POSTMODERN BERLIN,
IS REALM OF ETERNAL TIME, OF PURE SPIRIT, INHABITED
BY ANGELS. THE ANGELS CAN HEAR PEOPLE'S THOUGHTS
AND MOVE INSTANTANEOUSLY THROUGH SPACE. THEY ATTEMPT
TO INTERVENE IN WORLDLY AFFAIRS BY BATHING PEOPLE
IN SPIRITUAL VIBRATIONS. BUT OFTEN THEIR HELP FAILS.
THE YOUTH CONTEMPLATING SUICIDE JUMPS TO HIS DEATH.
YET, BOTH THE ANGELS AND SOME OF THE HUMANS ARE
AWARE OF EACH OTHER'S EXISTENCE, OF THE RADICAL
OTHERNESS OF EACH OTHER'S EXISTENCE.

Postmodern Environmentalism

Q **But how about in fields other than the arts? What impact has Postmodernism had on the real world?**

A Postmodern thought has even had an impact on the ecological movement—and thus upon mountains, redwoods, oceans, rivers and lakes. After all, Postmodernists are suspicious of grand narratives—of big stories—of utopian visions. And conservationists—the kind of people with "Save the River" bumper stickers—dream of a utopian ecological wilderness free of polluting industries.

The Postmodern tendency is to dismiss the concept of such a pure utopian wilderness as a grand narrative. And what's more, this big story is based on that evil of Poststructuralist evils—a binary opposition. In this case, the binary opposition wilderness/civilization.

But other environmentalists—especially those influenced by poet and eco-activist Gary Snyder—are acting out a philosophy that is both Postmodern and ecological,

SAVE ME
SAVE A TREE

instead of engaging in empty theorizing while the forests and rivers are suffering. Snyder's environmentalism is based on his long immersion in Zen Buddhist meditation and philosophy.

The Buddhist universe, like the Postmodern universe, is made up of countless heterogeneous selves with countless heterogeneous viewpoints. Not a utopia, based on one vision, but a heterotopia based on the visions of countless Others. And all of these Other selves—the selves of mountain lions, redwoods, rednecks, conservationists and rivers—are interconnected and mutually interdependent. And because none of these selves stand alone, by themselves, without all the Others, their separateness—their Otherness—is Empty, an Illusion.

Thus, like that Native American trickster figure, Coyote,

Snyder's poetic eco-philosophy dances around deconstructing the seeming "separate selves" of "wilderness" and "civilization." In practice, this means dancing between and weaving together ecological alliances between the "separate selves" of landowners, corporations, federal agencies, forests, mountains, mountain lions and frogs. It means, too, that we are all members of a mutual eating society. We both eat and are eaten. The eyes of the mountain lion stalking us are our own.

What is Postmodernism?
(In Retrospect)

Q So then, what **is** Postmodernism?

A According to Lyotard, it has to do with scepticism about Grand Narratives; and it is about heterogeneity. Ac-\cording to Jameson, it must involve a way of mapping the new and confusing contours of our late capitalistic times.

According to Baudrillard, Postmodernism is a flow of ultra-technological images in a consumerist hyperreality across a mediascape or mindscreen to which we can only passively surrender.

According to cyberpunk, it is a world dominated by multinational corporations and the data they control. Yet cyberpunks advocate a hacker ethic, tapping into and using such data for personal ends.

According to Charles Jencks, however, all these thinkers are only describing late capitalism or late modernism. Authentic Postmodernism, he argues, involves double coding the artistic representation of modernism with something else—some Other. For, as all Postmodern thinkers would admit, the world is shrinking. There is no one dominant worldview. Pluralism rules. Traditional, modern, late modern and Postmodern attitudes all rub elbows in the same culture.

This means that the Other increasingly encroaches upon what had once been our private space. So much of Postmodern thought has to do with this encroach-

ment of the Other—whether that Other is Other individuals, Other groups, Other species, Other races, the Other of "male," the Other of "the West," the Other of "Europe," the Other of the conscious mind, the Other of the rational mind, the Other of modernism, the Other **of** "ourself" or **in** "ourself."

Through double coding, Postmodern architecture, art and literature represent the Other, and thus present heterogene-

ity; by looking **backward** to the past, or **sideways** to a local culture. Thus, while using modernist techniques, they include the Other, humorously, ironically or playfully, rather than excluding it. This is why Jencks writes Post-modernism with a hyphen: because in these Postmodern times, there are a lot of hybrid identities. And this is something quite new. For, as we have discussed, in past centuries we looked for some Supermyth or messiah to unite all of humanity under the umbrella of one overarching philosophy. The Postmodern mind has given up such a hope. This has led to a radical change in how we believe.

We are forced to recognize that our world resists grand

narratives as much as individuals and groups crave them. That our world is a carnival of colorful and contradictory worldviews. We have come to realize that our view of reality isn't as real as it once seemed. We have come to realize that there is not one reality but many different, often conflicting realities. We have come to see that our ideas about truth are not eternal, but made. The ideas that the only God is Yahweh, or Allah, or the Goddess, or that some god named Bumba vomited the Moon and Stars, or the scientific notion that the Moon is a physical body of such and such mass that orbits another physical body, the planet Earth, of such and such a mass, in such and such an orbit that can be mathematically described, or that Western medicine is superior to Oriental herbalism, or that being feminine equals sugar and spice and everything nice, or that the Caucasian race is the masterrace—

all these are man-made notions. They are inventions—they are social constructs. Few people really believe anymore in an objective reality. And few believe that any one system of thought, any one big story or theory of mythic proportions, is capable of explaining everything. Not even science is objective—be-cause its data are always dependent on theory. Realities are social, linguistic constructions—useful fictions, relative perspectives.

If the grand narratives, the master narratives, the big stories, are no longer believable—if they have disappeared—they have been replaced by a hodge-podge of little narratives. Postmodern people, instead of dreaming of the day when all the world will be united under the universal banner of Marxism or

Christianity or Science, are more interested in seeing the world as a kind of carnival of cultures—a tribal gathering.

The shining sun of Universal Truth and Meaning is eclipsed by the colorful display of little dances, little stories. Big stories are replaced by little stories. Stories are no longer about an attempt to establish some sort of universal Utopia, unless it be a heterotopia. They do not try to prove themselves by making universal claims. A Postmodern storyteller may tell in one night the Grimms' fairy tale of Hansel and Gretel and the evil witch in the dark forest who lives in the gingerbread house, a Native American trickster tale of Coyote seducing the chief's daughter, and an ancient myth from India about the creation of the universe from a golden egg. The storyteller and the audience form a social bond, but it is the bonding of a heterogeneous society that can live with the incongruities, conflicts, and gaps between the various stories. This Postmodern society does not mind if one story says that the Moon and Stars were vomited forth, and another story proclaims that the moon and stars were created by God. Postmodern audiences don't demand that all the heterogeneous stories add up to some grand, global, universal total sense; instead, they celebrate the fact that it's OK to stop making so much sense. Because of the explosion of cultural messages, we are beginning to understand that not only our stories but also our rituals, religious dogmas, myths, gender roles, self concepts, beliefs, histories and theories are cultural, social inventions. We are beginning to realize that we live in a world of man-made signs and symbols, and we have begun to play around with those signs and symbols humorously and ironically so that we are not enslaved to them. This often means accepting a Grand Narrative, but having an ironic attitude toward it. Thus we may be a "quasi" fundamentalist Christian or Muslim or orthodox Jew or Catholic; we go to church or to the synagogue or the mosque, even though we may have some doubts about the metaphysical claims propounded there. We may believe that our particular vocabulary and ideas about truth have no special claim to reality. That people with other orientations may be just as oriented to their own reality. Just as often it means participating in more than one grand narrative—being a Buddhist Christian, for instance. The fragmentation of grand narratives under the pressure of multiple, local forces has liberated the concern for Others. Whereas modernist writers such as Conrad thought they could speak for Others—for the colonized, for Africans, for women, for the Orient—Postmodernism's emphasis on differance (irreconcilable difference) has allowed formerly silenced Others such as women, gays, blacks, orientals etc. to express their own stories in their own voices.

YOU BETTER DO IT MY WAY.

Q But is this really happening? Haven't these Postmodern times produced just as frequently what Baudrillard describes as a proliferation of myths of origin? Hasn't Postmodernism seen a multiplication of cults, such as Japan's Sarin Gas Sect? And since there are so many millions of people caught up in cults and sects and major religions, it seems as though there is a need for Grand Narratives and that the Postmodern era has even produced a proliferation of them. So how does one reconcile the Postmodern notions that people no longer believe in Grand Narratives, that Grand Narratives oppress and marginalize minorities, that there is no Big Picture, that there is no Deep Structure to reality (and that if there was, the human mind could not know it) with the fact that Grand Narratives are very much in evidence?

A Yes, that's true. The New Age movements of the '60s and '70s drew inspiration from a mixture of pop-psychedelic gurus such as Timothy Leary, rock-shamans such as Jim Morrison of the Doors, and mantra-chanting savants from India steeped in the **Bhagavad Gita**. Baby boomer spirituality, while often serious and eclectic, tended to be narcissistic and worshipful of authority figures.

Although many Generation X-ers reject the psychedelic-fueled communal hedonism of the Boomers, much of Generation X spirituality continues to circulate by means of images borrowed from pop and rock. Thus, in the same way that a big chunk of Boomer '60s spirituality depended on the image-mix of the Beatles and the Maharishi, in the '90s, public television elevated mythologist Joseph Campbell to the status of sainthood; MTV icons such as Madonna writhed to techno-beat tracks while dangling religious-chic fashion bangles such as cleavage-accenting rosaries; fashion designers drew inspiration from Hasidic Jewish traditionalism and Amish understatement; austere monastic chant CDs hit number one on the pop charts; angels became widely circulated images and a topic of talk shows; the highly publicized men's movement and goddess movement celebrated a return to paganism; Gothic spirituality

OF COURSE MY WAY IS EVERY WHICH-WAY

images of body-piercing, tattooing and S/M inundated MTV; and cyberpunk morphed into cybershamanism. Cybershamanism, or technoshamanism, by the way, is a technopagan attempt to create ancient shamanistic experiences of ecstasy (traditionally induced by chanting, drumming, dancing and the ingestion of psychoactive substances) through computerized fractal art, designer drugs, and repetitious music that fills the room like incense. Sometimes cybershamans even engage in toadlicking, a fad started by a rumor that ingesting the venom of a Colorado River toad is a good idea. The venom, however, is often fatally toxic.

Q **It seems that, in the same way as the modernists, we are trying to fill in the post-Nietzschean Void by inventing our own images and grand narratives. Are there any traditional grand narratives from other cultures that are capable of embracing difference?**

A Yes. Although the grand narratives of Christianity, Islam and Judaism have a difficult time dealing with differences, there are two major traditions—Buddhism and Hinduism—that can and do embrace the differences in our increasingly pluralistic world.

Buddhism is democratic, cool, practical, inexpensive, and (because the liberation of Tibet from China has become a hip cause) Buddhism is politically correct. Postmodern peoples and cultures live in a world of differences. Buddhism's philosophy of interdependence lets us see our differences as a vast interconnected web. In fact, the image Buddhists use to illustrate this is that of Indra's net. At each intersection of the strands of this vast net, which is the universe of different selves, is

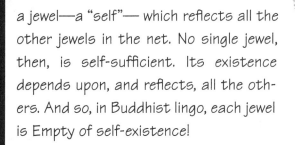

a jewel—a "self"— which reflects all the other jewels in the net. No single jewel, then, is self-sufficient. Its existence depends upon, and reflects, all the others. And so, in Buddhist lingo, each jewel is Empty of self-existence!

Q This sounds a lot like deconstruction. You remember the image of the face and the candle. Each are mutually interdependent. Neither can exist without the other.

A Yes. And a Buddhist would say, *"Both the faces and the candle are Empty of inherent existence!"*

Another tradition capable of accommodating differences is the Vedic tradition of India—Hinduism. Thousands of years ago the ancient Vedic seers proclaimed that *"Truth is One— but the sages call it by different names."* Thus Hindus tolerate a great variety of forms of worship and ways of attaining enlightenment.

References

Baudrillard, Jean

(A)   *Amerique.* (Paris: Grasset, 1986).

(SED)   *De la seduction.* (Paris: Galilee, 1980).

           The Ecstasy of Communication. Trans. Bernard and Caroline
           Schutze. (New York: Semiotext(e), 1988).

           For a Critique of the Political Economy of the Sign. Trans.
           Charles Levin. (St. Louis: Telos Press, 1981).

(FF)   *Forget Foucault.* Trans. Nicola Dufresne. (New York: Semiotext(e), 1987).

(SSM)   *In the Shadow of the Silent Majorities . . . or the End of the
           Social and Other Essays.* Trans. Paul Foss, Paul Patton and
           John Johnson. (New York: Semiotext(e), 1983).

(SIM)   *Simulations.* Trans. Nicola Dufresne. (New York: Semiotext(e) 1983).

           La societe de consommation. (Paris: Gallimard, 1970).

           Le systeme des objets. (Paris: Denoel-Gonthier, 1968).

Csicery-Ronay, Istavan

(SRS)   "Cyberpunk and Neuromanticism," in *Storming the Reality Studio,* Larry
           McCaffery, ed. (Durham: Duke Univ. Press, 184).

Deleuze, Gilles and Guattari, Felix

           Anti-Oedipus. Trans. Robert Hurley, Mark Seem, and Helen R. Lane, preface
           by Michel Foucault. (New York: Viking, 1977).

           Kafka: For a Minor Literature. Trans. Dana Polan. (Minneapolis: Univ. of
           Minnesota Press, 1986).

           'Rhizome.' Trans. Paul Foss and Paul Patton, *I and C 8* (1981): 49-71.

           A Thousand Plateaus: Capitalism and Schizophrenia. Trans. Brian Massumi.
           (Minneapolis: Univ. of Minnesota Press, 1987).

Derrida, Jacques

           Of Grammatology. Trans. Gayatri Spivak. (Baltimore: John UP, 1976).

Eco, Umberto

(PNR)   *Postscript to The Name of the Rose.* (New York and London: Harcourt
           Brace Jovanovich, 1984).

Foucault, Michel

           Discipline and Punish: The Birth of the Prison. Trans. Alan Sheridan. (New
           York: Pantheon, 1977).

           The History of Sexuality, Volume I: An Introduction. Trans. Robert Hurley.
           (New York: Pantheon, 1977).

           The Order of Things: An Archaeology of the Human Sciences. Trans. Alan
           Sheridan. (New York: Pantheon, 1970).

Gibson, William

(N)   *Neuromancer*. (New York: Ace, 1987).

Haraway, Donna

"A Cyborg Manifesto: Science, Technology, and Socialist Formation in the Late Twentieth Century," in *Simians, Cyborgs and Women: The Reinvention of Nature*. (New York: Routledge, 1991).

Harvey, David

The Condition of Postmodernity. (Blackwell: Oxford, 1990).

Hassan, Ihab

(TLP)   *The Dismemberment of Orpheus: Toward a Postmodern Literature*. (New York: Oxford Univ. Press, 1982).

Hemingway, Ernest

(SSEH)   *The Short Stories of Ernest Hemingway*. (New York: Scribner's, 1925).

Jameson, Fredric

(PCL)   "Postmodernism: or the Cultural Logic of Late Capitalism." *New Left Review*, 146 (1984): 53-92.

(PCS)   "Postmodernism and Consumer Society," In *Postmodern Culture*, Hal Foster, ed. (London and Sydney: 1985).

Lyotard, Jean Francois

(DF)   *Discours, figure*, Paris: Klincksieck, 1971.

(PC)   *The Postmodern Condition*, Trans. Bennington and Massumi. (Minneapolis: Univ. of Minnesota Press, 1984, first edition 1979).

Schwichtenberg, Cathy

(MPF)   "Madonna's Postmodern Feminism," in *The Madonna Connection*. Cathy Schwichtenberg, ed. (Boulder, CO: Westview Press, 1993).

Venturi, Robert; Scott Brown, Denise; and Izenour, Steven

(LLV)   *Learning from Las Vegas*. (Cambridge, Mass.: MIT Press, 1977).

Index

GESTALT FOR BEGINNERS ™
Sergio Sinay
Illustrated by Pable Blasberg
Translated by Mariana Solanet
ISBN 0-86316-258-4
(UK £7.99)

The origins of Gestalt Therapy derive from several sources, such as psychoanalysis by way of Wilhelm Reich and experimental Gestalt psychologists studying the nature of visual perception. It also includes field theorists such as Lewin and Humanist-Existential ideas that come primarily through the work of philosopher Martin Buber.

Gestalt, a German word with no exact equivalent in English, is usually translated as *form* or *shape*. Gestalt Therapy takes an holistic approach to healing and personal growth. It is a form of experiential

psychology that focuses on elements of the *here* and *now*. What we experience as we develop and how we adapt to that experience, come into the present as unresolved problems.

The purpose of Gestalt therapy is to teach people to work through and complete unresolved problems. Clients learn to follow their own ongoing process and to fully experience, accept and appreciate their complete selves.

Gestalt For Beginners ™ details the birth of the therapy, investigates the complex life of its creator Fitz Peris, and describes his revolutionary techniques such as the **Empty Chair**, the **Monodrama**, and the **Dream Studies**. The author also demonstrates why Gestalt Therapy is an ideal approach to self-affirmation and personal growth.

SAI BABA FOR BEGINNERS ™
Marcelo Berenstein
Illustrated by Miguel Angel Scenna
Translated by Mariana Solanet
ISBN 0-86316-257-6
(UK £7.99)

120million devotees worldwide recognise Sathya Sai Baba as a modern Hindu *avatr* (a human incarnation of the dicine) with the ability to be in various places simultaneously and with absolute knbowledge.

Why does this man claim to be God? Who gave him that title? And what did he come here for? **Sai Baba For Beginners** ™

details Sai Baba's life from his birth in 1926 to his studies, miracles, works, programme of education in human valor and his messages, up to the celebration of his recent 70th Birthday.

s new?

**THE HISTORY OF
CINEMA FOR
BEGINNERS ™**
Jarek Kupść
ISBN 0-86316-275-4
(UK £9.99)

The History of Cinema for Beginners™ is an informative introductory text on the history of narrative film and a reference guide for those who seek basic information on interesting movies. The book spans over one hundred years of film history, beginning with events leading up to the invention of the medium and chronicles the early struggle of the pioneers.

Readers are introduced to people behind and in front of the camera and presented with all major achievements of the silent and sound periods - even the most intangible film theories are explained and made easily digestible.

The unique aspect of **The History of Cinema For Beginners™** is its global approach to the subject of film history. The author introduces the reader to such significant developments as the Soviet montage, Italian neorealism, the French New Wave, the British kitchen sink cinema and the New German Film while providing a comprehensive coverage of American genre films such as slapstick comedy, the western, film noir, and science-fiction.

In addition, **The History of Cinema For Beginners™** invites the reader to delve into the lesser known regions of World cinema: Eastern Europe, South-East Asia, South America and others. The book also presents every key figure in the vast world of cinema with detailed information on his or her background, technique and major accomplishments. In a lighthearted manner, film makers such as D.W. Griffiths, Sergei Eisenstein and Orson Welles present their unique approach to movie making. The book's main goal is to make learning about movies as entertaining as it is watching them.

**POSTMODERNISM FOR
BEGINNERS ™**
Jim Powell
Illustrated by Joe Lee
ISBN 0-86316-139-1
(U.K. £7.99)

If you are like most people, you're not sure what Postmodernism is. And if this were like most books on the subject, it probably wouldn't tell you.

Besides what a few grumpy critics claim, Postmodernism is not a bunch of meaningless intellectual mind games. On the contrary, it is a reaction to the most profound spiritual and philosophical crises of our time -- the failure of the Enlightenment.

Jim Powell takes the position that Postmodernism is a series of *maps* that help people find their way through a changing world. **Postmodernism For Beginners** features the thoughts of Foucault on power and knowledge, Jameson on mapping the postmodern, Baudrillard on the media, Harvey on time-space compression, Derrida on deconstruction, and Deleuze and Guattari on rhizomes. The book also discusses postmodern artifacts such as Madonna, cyberpunk sci-fi, Buddhist ecology and teledildonics.

THE BODY FOR BEGINNERS ™
Dani Cavallaro.
Illustrated by Carline Vago
ISBN 0-86316-266-5
(U.K. £7.99)

What is the body? Is it a natural object? An idea? A word?

The Body For Beginners ™ addresses these and other questions by examining different aspects of the body in a variety of cultural situations. It argues that in recent years the body has been radically re-thought by both science and philosophy. Science has shown that it can be disassembled and restructured. Philosophy has challenged the traditional superiority of the mind over the body by stressing that corporeality is central to our experience and knowledge of the world.

Exploring the part played by the body in society, philosophy, the visual field and cyberculture and drawing examples from literature, cinema and popular culture, mythology and the visual arts, **The Body For Beginners** ™ suggests that there is no single way of defining the body. There are eating bodies, clothed bodies, sexual, erotic and pornographic bodies, medical bodies, technobodies, grotesque and hybrid bodies, tabooed, cannibalistic and vampiric bodies - to mention just a few of the aspects considered in this book.

No one map of the body is valid for all cultures. The word *body* will always mean something different, depending on the context in which it is used. This implies that the body can no longer be seen as a purely natural entity. In fact, it is a construct produced through various media, especially language.

All societies create images of the ideal body to define themselves. Framing the body is a vital means of establishing structures of power, knowledge, meaning and desire.
Yet, the body has a knack of breaking the frame. Its boundaries often turn out to be unstable. And this instability can be both scary and stimulating at the same time. This book will appeal to you if you are curious about the body as something more exciting and multi-faceted than simply a lump of meat!

october 1998

FANON FOR BEGINNERS ™
Deborah Wyrick, Ph.D.
ISBN 0-86316-255-X
(UK £7.99)

*Make me always a man
who questions - F. Fanon*

Philosopher, psychoanalyst, politician, prophet - Frantz Fanon (1925-1961) is one of the most influential writers on race and revolution. This book provides a clear, detailed introduction to the life and work of the man Jean-Paul Sartre called *the voice of the third world.*

Fanon For Beginners™ opens with a biography, following Fanon from his birthplace in Martinique, through combat in World War II and education in France, to his heroic involvement in the fights for Algerian independence and African decolonization. After a brief discussion of Fanon's political and cultural influences, the main section of the book covers the three principal stages of Fanon's thought:

The Search of Identity, as presented in *Black Skin, White Masks*, the stunning diagnosis of racism that Fanon wrote while studying medicine and psychoanalysis.

The Struggle Against Colonialism, as explained in *A Dying Colonialism* and *Towards the African Revolution*, essays Fanon produced when he was actively engaged in Algeria's war of independence.

The Process of Decolonization, as analysed in **The Wretched of the Earth**, the book that extended insights gained in Algeria to Africa and the Third World.

During his short lifetime Fanon accomplished a great deal, including writing books that have sold millions of copies throughout the world and continue to have a profound impact on contemporary cultural debate. **Fanon For Beginners** ™ concludes by examining Fanon's influence on political practice such as the Black Power Movement, literary theory, and post colonial studies.

How to get original thinkers to come to your home...

Orders:

U.K

For trade and credit card orders please contact our distributor:
Littlehampton Book Services Ltd,
10-14 Eldon Way, Littlehampton,
West Sussex, BN17 7HE
Phone Orders: 01903 828800
Fax Orders: 01903 828802
E-mail Orders:
orders@lbsltd.co.uk

Individual Orders: Please fill out the coupon below and send cheque or money order to:
Writers and Readers Ltd., 35
Britannia Row, London N1 8QH
Phone: 0171 226 3377
Fax: 0171 359 4554

U.S.

Please fill out the coupon below and send cheque or money order to:
Writers and Readers Publishing,
P.O. Box 461 Village Station,
New York NY 10014
Phone: (212) 982-3158
Fax: (212) 777 4924

Catalogue:
Or contact us for a FREE CATALOGUE of all our For Beginners titles

Name: _ _ _ _ _ _ _ _ _ _ _ _ _

_ _ _ _ _ _ _ _ _ _ _ _ _ _ _ _

Address: _ _ _ _ _ _ _ _ _ _ _

_ _ _ _ _ _ _ _ _ _ _ _ _ _ _ _

City: _ _ _ _ _ _ _ _ _ _ _ _ _ _

_ _ _ _ _ _ _ _ _ _ _ _ _ _ _ _

Postcode _ _ _ _ _ _ _ _ _ _ _
Tel:_ _ _ _ _ _ _ _ _ _ _ _ _ _ _
Access/ Visa/ Mastercard/ American
Express /Switch (circle one)
A/C No: _ _ _ _ _ _ _ _ _ _ _ _ _
Expires: _ _ _ _ _ _ _ _ _

ADDICTION & RECOVERY (£7.99)
ADLER (£7.99)
AFRICAN HISTORY (£7.99)
ARABS & ISRAEL (£7.99)
ARCHITECTURE (£7.99)
BABIES (£7.99)
BENJAMIN (£7.99)
BIOLOGY (£7.99)
BLACK HISTORY (£7.99)
BLACK HOLOCAUST (£7.99)
BLACK PANTHERS (£7.99)
BLACK WOMEN (£7.99)
BODY (£7.99)
BRECHT (£7.99)
BUDDHA (£7.99)
CASATNEDA (£7.99)
CHE (£7.99)
CHOMSKY (£7.99)
CLASSICAL MUSIC (£7.99)
COMPUTERS (£7.99)
THE HISTORY OF CINEMA (£9.99)
DERRIDA (£7.99)
DNA (£7.99)
DOMESTIC VIOLENCE (£7.99)
THE HISTORY OF EASTERN EUROPE (£7.99)
ELVIS (£7.99)
ENGLISH LANGUAGE (£7.99)
EROTICA (£7.99)
FANON (£7.99)
FOOD (£7.99)
FOUCAULT (£7.99)
FREUD (£7.99)
GESTALT (£7.99)
HEALTH CARE (£7.99)
HEIDEGGER (£7.99)
HEMINGWAY (£7.99)
ISLAM (£7.99)

HISTORY OF CLOWNS (£7.99)
I CHING (£7.99)
JAZZ (£7.99)
JEWISH HOLOCAUST (£7.99)
JUDAISM (£7.99)
JUNG (£7.99)
KIERKEGAARD (£7.99)
KRISHNAMURTI (£7.99)
LACAN (£7.99)
MALCOLM X (£7.99)
MAO (£7.99)
MARILYN (£7.99)
MARTIAL ARTS (£7.99)
MCLUHAN (£7.99)
MILES DAVIS (£7.99)
NIETZSCHE (£7.99)
OPERA (£7.99)
PAN-AFRICANISM (£7.99)
PHILOSOPHY (£7.99)
PLATO (£7.99)
POSTMODERNISM (£7.99)
STRUCTURALISM&
POSTSTRUCTURALISM (£7.99)
PSYCHIATRY (£7.99)
RAINFORESTS (£7.99)
SAI BABA (£7.99)
SARTRE (£7.99)
SAUSSURE (£7.99)
SCOTLAND (£7.99)
SEX (£7.99)
SHAKESPEARE (£7.99)
STANISLAVSKI (£7.99)
UNICEF (£7.99)
UNITED NATIONS (£7.99)
US CONSTITUTION (£7.99)
WORLD WAR II (£7.99)
ZEN (£7.99)

Individual Order Form   (clip out or copy complete page)

Book title	Quantity	Amount
	SUB TOTAL:	
U.S. only N.Y. RESIDENTS ADD 8 1/4 SALES TAX:		
Shipping & Handling ($3.00 for the first book; £.80 for each additional book):		
	TOTAL	